Imperial Cities
and the Reformation

BERND MOELLER

Imperial Cities
and the Reformation

THREE ESSAYS

Edited and translated by

H. C. ERIK MIDELFORT and MARK U. EDWARDS, JR.

THE LABYRINTH PRESS
Durham, North Carolina

These essays are translated from the German by permission of the author and the publishers. "Problems of Reformation Research" ("Probleme der Reformationsgeschichtsforschung") and "The German Humanists and the Beginnings of the Reformation" ("Die deutschen Humanisten und die Anfänge der Reformation") appeared in the *Zeitschrift für Kirchengeschichte,* Vierte Folge, 14 (1965): 246-57 and 8 (1959): 46-61 respectively. "Imperial Cities and the Reformation"(*Reichsstadt und Reformation*) was published in the series Schriften des Vereins für Reformationsgeschichte, No. 180 (Gütersloher Verlagshaus Gerd Mohn, 1962).

Library of Congress Cataloging in Publication Data
Moeller, Bernd, 1931-
    Imperial cities and the Reformation.

    Translation of: Reichsstadt und Reformation, with two other essays.

    Reprint. Originally published: Philadelphia: Fortress Press, 1972.

    Contents: Problems of Reformation research—The German humanists and the beginnings of the Reformation—Imperial cities and the Reformation.

    1. Reformation—Germany—Addresses, essays, lectures. 2. Imperial cities (Holy Roman Empire)—Addresses, essays, lectures. 3. Renaissance—Germany—Addresses, essays, lectures. 4. Reformation—Historiography—Addresses, essays, lectures. I. Midelfort, H. C. Erik. II. Edwards, Mark U. III. Title.

BR307.M613 1982   274.3′06   82-6600
ISBN 0-939464-04-7 (pbk.)   AACR2

Printed in the United States of America

Contents

ABBREVIATIONS

Bucer:

DS   —*Deutsche Schriften*, 3 vols.
        (Gütersloh and Paris, 1960–1964).

De Regno—*Martini Buceri Opera Latina,* ed. F. Wendel
 Christi   (Paris and Gütersloh, 1955).

Luther:

WA   —*D. Martin Luthers Werke.* Kritische Gesamtausgabe
        (Weimar, 1883–   ).

WA, Br —*D. Martin Luthers Werke.* Briefwechsel
        (Weimar, 1930–   ).

WA, TR —*D. Martin Luthers Werke.* Tischreden
        (Weimar, 1912–1921).

LW   —American Edition of *Luther's Works*
        (Philadelphia and St. Louis, 1955–   ).

Zwingli:

ZW-CR   —*Huldreich Zwinglis Sämtliche Werke,* vols. 88 ff. of the
        Corpus Reformatorum
        (Leipzig, 1905–   ).

ZW-Sch —*Huldreich Zwinglis Werke,* ed. M. Schuler and
        J. Schulthess, 8 vols.
        (Zurich, 1828–1842).

Introduction

The Reformation of the sixteenth century has become the subject of intense research in the last generation. Investigators ferret in the remotest hinterlands for material on the religious revival; Luther research alone is a flourishing enterprise; and scholars pursue the minor reformers of small German towns with a vigor and sense of purpose that are remarkable, to say the least. Masses of data have been compiled. All of this industrious research, however, has thrown very little light on the Reformation as a whole or on its place in European history. Interest in the theology of the fifteenth and sixteenth centuries has been intense and exciting, but scholars in the field have chosen to treat the Reformation as an isolated phenomenon, and to ignore the political, sociological, and philosophical matrix in which it developed. Nowhere is this more the case than in Germany where the separation of political and social history from theology has become a scholarly way of life.

It is therefore a most welcome event when a German historian undertakes to place the Reformation in the context of secular history. For the past fifteen years Professor Bernd Moeller has been trying to do just that. Relating reformers and their ideas to the social and political world in which they lived, Moeller's work has been truly stimulating and seminal, and even American scholars have begun to draw inspiration from it. Hence, the publication of three essays by Moeller, presented here for the first time in English, is an occasion of some importance for those who do not read

German. They will discover some of the reasons why Bernd Moeller is one of the foremost Reformation historians at work in Germany today.

His first essay is a striking appeal to his colleagues to descend from the misty heights of systematic theology and to approach the Reformation as a unique, alien, historical event.[1] Instead of presuming that they are the first to understand what Luther really meant, scholars should consider the impact that Luther and the other reformers made in their own day, and how their contemporaries were able to apprehend their teachings. Furthermore, Moeller calls for an approach in which Luther's teachings are no longer the standard by which all Reformation theology is measured. This means that we must turn to the minor figures of the sixteenth century and study them sympathetically.

The two essays that follow present several examples of this new approach to the Reformation. In his essay on "The German Humanists and the Beginnings of the Reformation,"[2] Moeller shows how fruitful it can be to look beyond the great humanists like Erasmus. Traditional scholarship has seen the controversy between Erasmus and Luther as a laboratory case of the conflict between Renaissance and Reformation, but Moeller shows how much more complex the situation actually was. First, an analysis of the German humanist movement shows that it did not consist of a unified group, but of at least two groups divided by age.[3] The famous humanists of Luther's day, including Erasmus, belonged to an older generation of scholars who ultimately shrank back from Luther's radical break with the Roman church. The younger humanists, like Melanchthon, however, gave Luther his first support, and continued to support his cause even when it involved great personal risks. Moeller has suggested, in other words, that there is a generational conflict, perhaps even a "generation gap,"

1. Bernd Moeller, "Probleme der Reformationsgeschichtsforschung," *Zeitschrift für Kirchengeschichte* 76 (1965): 246–57.
2. Bernd Moeller, "Die deutschen Humanisten und die Anfänge der Reformation," *Zeitschrift für Kirchengeschichte* 70 (1959): 46–61.
3. On this point cf. Lewis W. Spitz, *The Religious Renaissance of the German Humanists* (Cambridge, Mass.: Harvard University Press, 1963).

between those who supported Luther and those for whom his message had no appeal.[4]

In the third essay Moeller attacks the problem of "Imperial Cities and the Reformation."[5] The fact that most of the imperial cities harbored Protestant movements, and that many of them became officially Protestant, has never before been carefully considered. Moeller describes the ways in which these late-medieval cities were prepared for the Reformation, and what is more important, advances a theory to explain why the imperial cities of south-western Germany were attracted to Zwingli's Reformation while the northern cities were content with Luther. His explanation is not simply that Luther lived in the North and Zwingli in the South, but that a characteristic moral attitude in the southern towns (including those of Switzerland) made them welcome the morally disciplined Reformation of Zwingli and Bucer. Such an analysis even enables us to understand in a new way the vigorous debate over the Eucharist during the 1520s and after. This debate seems to have depended in part on differing conceptions of community. Zwingli's conception of a communal, memorial Eucharist could take root only in soil prepared for it by that general concern for moral community characteristic of the southern towns.

Thanks to Moeller's work a new picture of the Reformation emerges in which theology is seen in the context of political and social history. In a broad sense, Moeller's work confronts the questions raised recently by the sociologist, Guy Swanson.[6] However, instead of arguing that the German Reformation can be reduced to differing views of the state, Moeller presents a fully

4. For a continuation of this theme, cf. Lewis W. Spitz, "The Third Generation of German Renaissance Humanists," in *Aspects of the Renaissance,* ed. Archibald R. Lewis (Austin, Tex.: University of Texas Press, 1967), pp. 105–21.

5. Bernd Moeller, *Reichsstadt und Reformation,* Schriften des Vereins für Reformationsgeschichte, No. 180 (Gütersloh: Gerd Mohn, 1962).

6. Guy Swanson, *Religion and Regime: A Sociological Account of the Reformation* (Ann Arbor, Mich.: University of Michigan Press, 1967); for the continuing debate, cf. Theodor V. Brodek, Natalie Z. Davis, H. G. Koenigsberger, and Guy E. Swanson, "Reevaluating the Reformation: A Symposium," *The Journal of Interdisciplinary History* 1, no. 3 (Spring, 1971): 379–446.

historical analysis. He shows that the Reformation was embedded in the political history of Germany, but recognizes at the same time the great moral and religious influence of the reformers. It is along these lines that Moeller's work speaks to one of the current controversies of American Reformation research. His theory, extensively documented, will continue to provoke scholarly activity for the next generation.

Moeller's work has naturally prompted new research in Germany too,[7] and Professor Moeller himself is painfully aware that these three essays no longer represent the latest word. As brilliant and seminal articles, however, they deserve to be widely known.

After so much by way of introduction to the essays, what should be said of their author? Born in 1931 in Berlin, Moeller studied theology and history at the University of Mainz. His doctoral dissertation in 1956 was a study of Tauler. From 1956 on he has been concerned with Reformation history, first as an assistant at the University of Heidelberg where he worked with Professor Freiherr von Campenhausen. His *Habilitationsschrift* appeared in 1961 on the subject of Johann Zwick and the Reformation in Constance.[8] From 1958 to 1964 Moeller was *Privatdozent* at Heidelberg. In 1964 he was called as professor of church history to the University of Göttingen. At present he enjoys the honor of being rector of that university.

7. See the following articles by Moeller: "Frömmigkeit in Deutschland um 1500," *Archiv für Reformationsgeschichte* 56 (1965): 5–31; "Augustana-Studien," *Archiv für Reformationsgeschichte* 57 (1966): 76–95; "Zur Reformationsgeschichte," *Verkündigung und Forschung* H. 1 (1968): 65–95; "Zwinglis Disputationen. Studien zu den Anfängen der Kirchenbildung und des Synodalwesens im Protestantismus. I. Teil," *Zeitschrift der Savigny-Stiftung für Rechtsgeschichte, Kanonistische Abteilung* 56 (1970): 275–324. Other research is following the lines of Ernst W. Kohls, "Evangelische Bewegung und Kirchenordnung in oberdeutschen Reichsstädten," *Zeitschrift der Savigny-Stiftung für Rechtsgeschichte, Kanonistische Abteilung* 84 (1967): 110–34. A brief survey of recent trends may be found in Harold J. Grimm, "The Reformation and the Urban Social Classes in Germany," in John C. Olin, James D. Smart, and Robert E. McNally, S. J., *Luther, Erasmus and the Reformation: A Catholic-Protestant Reappraisal* (New York: Fordham University Press, 1969), pp. 75–86.

8. Bernd Moeller, *Johannes Zwick und die Reformation in Konstanz*, Quellen und Forschungen zur Reformationsgeschichte, vol. 28 (Gütersloh: Gerd Mohn, 1961).

Introduction

With regard to the translations: the first two essays were translated from the original German. The third essay, on "Imperial Cities and the Reformation," however, was translated from the expanded French version of 1966.[9] In the course of this translation the many errors that marred that translation have been corrected. The notes to "Imperial Cities and the Reformation" presented a problem because of their length and the inclusion of a large number of quotations from primary sources. For reasons of economy and readability these notes have been cut by about a third. The notes that have been kept, however, indicate well the range and type of Moeller's source material.

H. C. Erik Midelfort

Mark U. Edwards, Jr.

9. Bernd Moeller, *Villes d'Empire et réformation,* trans. Albert Chenou, Travaux d'histoire éthico-politique, no. 10 (Geneva: Librairie Droz, 1966).

Publisher's Note:

Since the preceding introduction was written in 1972, Bernd Moeller has remained as professor of Church History in the University of Göttingen, though he is no longer rector. Debate about his work has continued in scholarly books and journals from 1972 to the present. English-speaking students of the Reformation may orient themselves to this debate by reading Steven E. Ozment, *The Reformation in the Cities* (New Haven, 1975); Robert W. Scribner, "Is there a Social History of the Reformation?" *Social History* 4 (1977), 483-505; Thomas A. Brady, *Ruling Class, Regime and Reformation at Strassburg, 1520-1555* (Leiden, 1977); *The Urban Classes, the Nobility and the Reformation: Studies in the Social History of the Reformation in England and Germany,* edited by Wolfgang J. Mommsen, Peter Alter and Robert W. Scribner (Stuttgart, 1979); and E. William Monter, "Reformation History and Social History," *Archive for Reformation History* 72 (1981), 5-12.

Problems of
Reformation Research

Problems of Reformation Research

A careful study of recent Reformation research in Germany is certain to disclose a peculiar fact. Except in Göttingen and several other enlightened places, nontheological, German-speaking historians have tended to ignore the period from 1500 to 1650. In our attempts to understand this period historically we have come to question the old dividing lines between the ages. We now understand in theory the difficulties inherent in the disputes over the limits of the Middle Ages, and we can see the complex overlapping of periods, in contrast with the beginnings of the Middle Ages, where the boundaries are still more or less clear. Most medievalists still believe, however, that their task of teaching and research encounters an iron curtain at the year 1500. Modern historians, on the other hand, begin their studies with the year 1650. This is the date at which, with the end of the Wars of Religion, rational factors begin to dominate European history. With a few important exceptions, nontheological historians, especially Protestants, have treated the intervening century and a half as a sort of no man's land.

This has had various implications for historical studies. Dissertations are seldom written on this period, professorial theses almost never. For the most part, research is at a standstill. No wide-ranging and ambitious monographs like Gerhard Ritter's *Luther* or Karl Brandi's *Charles V* have appeared for more than a quarter of a century. Furthermore, in a portion of those works that *have* appeared we find an increasing tendency to treat history as though it were an antiquarian exercise. It comes down to saying with Count Yorck, "Dust to dust."

While it is not our wish to examine and explain this state of affairs in detail, some things at least are clear. This trend cannot be casually explained away. Widespread shifts in what historians consider important are usually a reflection of the relationship that exists between the historical period and the present. I suspect therefore that the neglect of the Reformation by secular historians and, as Ebeling noted, "the forgetting of Luther . . . by today's educated man"[1] reflect the same underlying cause, the widespread and basic uncertainty we feel toward the Reformation and its historical outgrowths.

Probably the most important reason for this neglect is the difficulty one finds in dealing with the Reformation objectively. Even the modern observer can scarcely remain unaffected by the enormous tensions of the period. Luther made unprecedented spiritual demands upon his age and tore it apart. The cleavages he initiated stretched across generations and peoples and led to massacres and wars of proportions previously inconceivable. It is much easier to remain detached or to like some aspects and dislike others in dealing with the Middle Ages or the period of absolutism.

Furthermore, we are now aware of the profound spiritual difference between the Reformation and the modern age. Despite diverse accents, starting points, and interpretations, most theologians, including Friedrich Gogarten, have adopted the conclusions of Troeltsch or Dilthey rather than those of Holl.[2] Whatever the relationship of this new historical point of view to the profound break in modern man's self-awareness, historians and the educated man in search of self-understanding can now easily neglect or ignore the Reformation period. I question whether this view is fully justified and whether the resulting approach can be continued in the long run. Since I lack sufficient expertise in this area, however, I must now let the matter rest.

1. G. Ebeling, *Luther. Einführung in sein Denken* (Tübingen, 1964), p. 9.
2. In any case according to H. Fischer, *Neue Zeitschrift für systematische Theologie* 5 (1963): 167 ff.

Although nontheological historians have withdrawn from Reformation research, the field has not gone to seed. Theologians, who have always for obvious and legitimate reasons worked energetically and profitably in the area, have not abandoned it. On the contrary, theological Reformation research has increased extraordinarily in extent and intensity and is today more wide-ranging than ever before. In theology, especially in Protestantism, Reformation history has become a focal point of interest.

In the decades before World War I, Harnack, Loofs, and Reinhold Seeberg, Karl Müller, and Albert Hauck depicted ecclesiastical and theological development in all its breadth and complexity. They wrote powerful, panoramic works that spanned the ages and made their time the great period of Protestant church history. Since then Protestant church historians have nearly ceased working in such eras as the Middle Ages and vast segments of the modern period. Panoramic outlines on a par with the earlier works in range of conception and in sophistication of detail are no longer appearing. Instead, attention and effort have been concentrated for the most part on two eras: the patristic period and the Reformation.

We see here a development quite opposite to what we saw in nontheological history. And even though this trend did not completely reject the directions established by church historians up to 1914,[3] still it is clear that it was primarily determined by *external* factors. The earthshaking breakup in German Protestant theology around 1920 affected church history more than any other theological discipline. A huge chasm separates the church historian Harnack, the greatest theologian of the older period, and the dogmatician Barth, the greatest theologian of the modern period. Harnack, while moving his library, contemptuously labeled the section of dogmatic works "belles lettres,"[4] while Barth, not mean-

---

3. For example, E. Troeltsch commented as early as 1901 in his review in the *Göttingische Gelehrte Anzeigen* of the second volume of Seeberg's *History of Dogma*: "We will not have need of another general history of dogma for some time. On the other hand, we have now even more need for detailed monographs on individuals and especially on particular constellations of ideas"; *Gesammelte Schriften*, Vol. 4: *Aufsätze zur Geistesgeschichte und Religionssoziologie* (Tübingen, 1925), p. 752.
4. Agnes von Zahn-Harnack, *Adolf von Harnack*, 2nd ed. (Berlin, 1951), p. 83.

ing to express a value judgment of course, described church history as an "indispensable aid to exegetical, dogmatic, and practical theology."[5] In the interval between these two comments there had come about a realization that the Christian message transcends the ages. Theology was thereby freed from the confines to which historicism had seemed to consign it. With respect to the proper theme and task of theology, church history and historical understanding per se became "dreadfully irrelevant."[6] History had lost its creative significance and came to be used primarily as a source of theological opinions and lessons. This largely explains the pre-occupation with the patristic and Reformation periods. It was primarily from *these* periods that theologians could expect to draw example and inspiration.

No serious Protestant church historian of today can blithely deny the value of this approach which, with various modifications, has become generally established in German Protestant theology. Nor can he simply return to the earlier framework by denying the new or newly accented theological perceptions that determine this recent approach. That the church is defined by its tie to Christ and that faith is indemonstrable and unmediated, are presuppositions that will have to be taken into account in church history research.

We are also indebted to and bound by the work of the past decades because we can see the impressive, scholarly results that were achieved in Reformation research. There was even a significant change in methodology: the original texts have become the center of scholarly interest, and the attempt is at least made to make their original meaning the methodological standard of judgment.

The most important result of this new approach is a change in our picture of Luther. We see the Reformer in the profound and concentrated tension of his thought as wholly a theologian. He has lost all heroic features. We have come to understand the meaning

---

5. K. Barth, *Die kirchliche Dogmatik,* vol. I, part 1, 6th ed. (Zollikon-Zurich, 1952), p. 3.
6. A comment made by K. Barth in 1916 in one of his early letters to Thurneysen; *Antwort. Karl Barth zum 70. Geburtstag* (Zollikon-Zurich, 1956), p. 845.

of *Anfechtung* for his theology and faith and to understand in this light that his discovery of the gospel was a discovery of the God-given means of consolation. His appropriation of traditional dogma and his thoughtful interpretation of Christology appear therefore as central elements of his doctrine. We now see his understanding of the church as clearly a tension between the medieval instrument of salvation and the modern congregation. We have come to emphasize the crucial theological and spiritual reasons for his escape from the sacramental shell of the Middle Ages, and for his new, free, objective attitude toward worldly things, and finally for his new conception of nature, history, and society.

Along with the intensification of Luther studies and the clarification of our understanding of Luther, the last decades saw an upsurge in research on Anabaptism that almost became a vogue. These decades were, however, especially marked by a lively concern with the reformers who accompanied and supported Luther. These studies have given us a significantly clearer conception of the theological relationship between Luther and Zwingli, Bucer and numerous other lesser leaders of the Reformation. Above all we now have a better grasp of the theological characteristics of Melanchthon.

No matter how welcome and useful these and other achievements of recent research, we cannot be satisfied with the total picture. Perhaps it is not an exaggeration to speak of a contemporary crisis in theological Reformation research. To put it in a nutshell, it seems that we are threatened with losing the Reformation as an event in *church* history.

In the last decades our research has been concentrated almost exclusively on Reformation *theology*. The reasons for this have already been touched on. Consequently, we have frequently lost sight of the Reformation as history, as an event of the distant past, and as a complex network of historical relationships. In doing so we may well have oversimplified both our conception and evaluation of Reformation theology itself. After all, this theology had such a great impact in history precisely because it was intricately interwoven into history. The accusation is sometimes made today, especially by Marxist historians, that "the dominant direction of Reformation history and theology in West Germany is profoundly ahistorical" and amounts to a "flight from history."[7] The theological observer need not accept the underlying Marxist notion of history, which is no less one-sided and ahistorical, but he cannot entirely reject such accusations. Much of the stature and profundity of twentieth-century Protestant theology may be due primarily to the renewed interest in the Reformation. But it is also possible that some of the failures and errors that accompanied the Protestant renewal are due to the way we have come to regard the Reformation.

I think that Reformation research itself has been affected by two problematic developments. As already noted, contemporary *Luther research* has become "almost a branch of systematic theology."[8] As a matter of fact, the critical observer cannot escape the impression that this area of research is one of the battlefields where contemporary theological schools air their differences. While there is agreement today on some guidelines for a theological interpretation of Luther, there still exist great differences on particular issues, especially where contemporary Protestantism itself is struggling for clarity.

An example is the recent debate about the relationship that Luther saw between the worldly and divine kingdoms, a debate characterized, not without justice, as a "maze."[9] We find similar disagreement on other topics, especially those bearing on the genuinely important question of the exact nature and date of Luther's Reformation discovery, the so-called tower experience. This, by the way, was already a hotly disputed question before 1914. Of course, one must not overlook the fact that one aspect of this debate is more concerned with specific interpretation of early Luther texts than with their general evaluation. Moreover, one must admit that profound differences of opinion continue to exist

7. M. Steinmetz, in *Die frühbürgerliche Revolution in Deutschland,* ed. G. Brendler (Berlin, 1961), p. 32.
8. R. Stupperich, *Archiv für Kulturgeschichte* 43 (1961): 377–92.
9. J. Heckel, *Im Irrgarten der Zwei-Reichelehre* (Munich, 1957).

over the origin and essence of the Reformation. As a result, the traditional confessional lines have been thoroughly confused. While differing in the details of their arguments, a large number of researchers, ranging from ecumenical Catholics such as Lortz and Iserloh to K. A. Meissinger [Lutheran] and all the way to [Calvinist] Ernst Bizer, consider the so-called young Luther as still more or less "Catholic" in the years up to about 1518. They argue that Reformation theology proper appears only in the later period. This interpretation finds its most extreme antithesis in the position held, nearly alone, by East German Professor Rosemarie Müller-Streisand.[10] She interprets the young Luther as the genuine Protestant, who in the year 1518 began his great defection back to Catholicism.

It seems obvious that dogmatics, which neglects historical understanding, has had too much influence on Luther research. It is significant, too, that the recent commentary on the Lutheran confessional writings was written for the most part by dogmaticians rather than by church historians. What Old or New Testament scholar would allow this in his field? It seems that scholars are asking Luther many inappropriate questions and are forcing answers from him that he is not willing to give. When dealing with the Reformation, scholars do not always properly allow for the enormous distance of more than four centuries and the profound changes in thought and conditions that have taken place. In our period we have heard the cry "God is dead" and have had to deal with secularization, historicism, historical-critical research, and the "complete subjectifying of reality"[11] with a related intensifying of the problem of certainty, to list only a few examples. If we think we can relate directly to a period where all this was not the case, we simply fool ourselves. This is true even if many of these changes were anticipated in Luther's thought and to some extent in his intentions. The general loss of the historical dimension often leads to the enthronement of Luther's theology as a sort of peren-

10. It had forerunners in the older liberal theology, e.g., Hermann Barge.
11. F. Gogarten, in *Anfänge der dialektischen Theologie*, ed. J. Moltmann, vol. 2 (Munich, 1963), p. 202.

nial theology. Strictly speaking this makes as little sense in theology as it does in history.

This treatment of the Reformation along narrow dogmatic lines entails a second problem for Reformation historical research. Not only is Luther himself taken and interpreted as norm and authority for the contemporary needs of theology and church, but German Protestants have come to evaluate the theology and history of the *Reformation as a whole* in terms of an exalted and almost canonical Luther. Now here too we cannot simply deny the basic justice of such a view. Since we more clearly recognize Luther's theological profundity and breadth of vision than did earlier generations, we are particularly struck by the decline in theological sophistication among Lutherans after Luther's death. We have developed precise methods and a keen eye for spotting differences between specific theological expressions. We can analyze Luther's gradual escape from the tangled web of late scholastic theology; his opposition to humanism and the permanent gap between him and the reformers with a humanistic background, which is to say almost all the others; and finally the apparent decline of the Lutheran church and its theology after the death of the Reformer.

Regardless of how little exception we might take to these works individually, the total picture of the Reformation offered by most of them is simply incredible. It may well be that the new tendencies in research have separated us from historical "reality" rather than brought us closer. For if we put the results of these works together, we must conclude that Luther's own intentions were totally or almost totally misunderstood in his day and that the later history of Protestantism shows "an unprecedented historical discontinuity," which can indeed raise questions about "divine providence in the history of theology."[12]

Lately one could even get the impression that Luther himself did not understand his own position. A recent work[13] would have

12. K. Barth in letters of 1924; *Gottesdienst—Menschendienst. Eduard Thurneysen zum 70. Geburtstag* (Zollikon-Zurich, 1958), pp. 99, 103.
13. For the following viewpoint I am indebted to E. Bizer's critical review of R. Schäfer, *Christologie und Sittlichkeit in Melanchthons frühen Loci* (1961) in *Evangelische Theologie* 24 (1964): 1–24.

10

us believe that in the period when Melanchthon had the closest contact with Luther, they really remained worlds apart. And so Luther's well-known sympathies for his friend's doctrine, which reached its high point as late as 1537 in the striking slogan: "Substance and eloquence = Philip; eloquence without substance = Erasmus; substance without eloquence = Luther; neither substance nor eloquence = Carlstadt,"[14] can only be interpreted as a first-class case of misunderstanding oneself. Modern theologians must pay a price for the pride that leads them to boast that they are the first men in history really to understand the essence of Luther. That price is the loss of the Reformation as an event in church history and the reduction of the Protestant movement in the sixteenth century to *one* man—Luther.

This harsh verdict, perhaps overly harsh, presents a painful challenge to the impetuous critic. For I myself am immersed in current research and indebted to it at every point. I should find ways to avoid these difficulties and should replace what is good by what is better. I cannot expect to meet adequately these demands with the following aphorisms, which merely suggest a few major tasks and a few specialized projects.

We can summarize our basic criticism of contemporary theological Reformation research in one sentence. Reformation research has obviously not sufficiently recognized the underlying fact that its subject matter is a historical event which connects past and future under absolutely specific, unique, and irretrievable circumstances. It is an event which is foreign to us and cannot be repeated. It is characterized by a factual situation that cannot be deduced. In the last analysis, it involves a complex of historical relations which we cannot penetrate. Finally, we interpreters have both the advantage and disadvantage of living after the event. The common desire of modern Protestant theology to take seriously the historical nature of Christian existence has had negligible impact on our conception of the Reformation. It has not sharpened our ability to understand history at all.

In closing I shall attempt to illustrate what I mean and suggest

14. *WA*, TR 3:619.

ways out of the difficulties. In doing so, I shall cite several examples from the early Reformation, with which I am most familiar.

1. As we have already mentioned, in recent decades one of the important and lasting accomplishments of the history of theology has been the examination of how Luther worked through the dense and burdensome web of late medieval theology. Of course these penetrating investigations, which began with Ernst Wolf's *Staupitz und Luther* and continue up to the present, have certainly not completely explained this difficult process. But they have laid bare its complexity, interconnections, and depth. Yet there remain here many tasks for research. We have nearly lost sight of the historical problems of the *relationship of the Reformation as a whole to the Middle Ages*. This is the question of how Europe was made ready for the Reformation, of how the Reformation broke away from the Middle Ages, and of how the Middle Ages survived within the Reformation.

Although Luther research has discounted the influence of pre-reformers, it has not affected the conclusion that the ground was prepared in other ways for Luther's victory. However, as we are progressively realizing, the religious and spiritual condition of Germany on the eve of the Reformation did not resemble a powder keg needing only Luther's appearance to spark an explosion, as scholars used to think. Thus the materialistic conception of history, including the works by Rosemarie Müller-Streisand, distorts and coarsens the historical facts when it insists that the primary, central reason for Luther's victory was men's hatred for the medieval church, and when it regards Luther as primarily an ecclesiastical critic. In any event, by the end of the Middle Ages Germany was at least as faithful to the church and as "medieval" as the surrounding kingdoms, where the Reformation did not occur. And piety was associated, if anything, more closely with holy *things* than in earlier periods. Yet clearly this did not later prevent anti-ceremonial aspects of Protestant sermons from striking fire. We are far from understanding this tangle of historical threads. And we have scarcely come to terms with the most basic, incongruous, and unprecedented aspect of the whole Reformation: that it was a theologian who unleashed a revolution in world history and forced his rule on that revolution, and, what is more, that he was the most profound of all the theologians.

2. In view of the "great complexity of hermeneutics"[15] we should not delude ourselves into thinking that *Luther* research can entirely avoid the "narrow dogmatic treatment" sketched above. Yet at least scholars should be more aware of the problems and should *want* to avoid them.

It is probably necessary to correct our image of Luther in several important ways. To caricature the common description, Luther generally appears as a great sage, a kind of spiritual colossus, who attains his Reformation breakthrough, draws the broad consequences, and then drags people with him as he strides through history handing out his truths right and left. Recently we have begun to realize that such a view is a distortion. I find particularly suggestive Heinrich Bornkamm's recent remarks on the part played by "dialogue" in Luther's writings.[16] He shows that throughout the enormous corpus of his works Luther always says what he has to say through dialogue with a partner who instructs and enriches or argues and disagrees, who vacillates or questions, is excited or reserved.

We should take more seriously these observations as well as Ebeling's remark that Luther was "uniquely responsive to events."[17] They should serve as heuristic principles even in considering the development of Luther's thought. And we will have to recognize that Luther's theology began with a dialogue with Paul, that has been completely mistitled the "tower experience." And it developed less by elaborating principles realized in one insight than by confronting the most diverse challenges in lively debate. This approach should clarify much of the theological development, vacillation, inconsistency, and contradiction found in Luther. It seems to

15. G. Ebeling, in his article, "Luther: II," in *Die Religion in Geschichte und Gegenwart,* ed. Kurt Galling, vol. 4, 3rd ed. (Tübingen, 1960), col. 496.
16. H. Bornkamm, "Luther als Schriftsteller," *Sitzungsberichte der Heidelberger Akademie der Wissenschaften,* philologisch-historische Klasse, no. 1 (1965), p. 29.
17. Ebeling, "Luther: II," col. 507.

me that Luther's theology also has structural affinity to that of Paul, as presented in recent New Testament scholarship. Luther research could probably learn a great deal from the most recent Pauline research. For example, the common concern in biblical scholarship for the "vital context" or *Sitz im Leben* of a text should also become a concern of Reformation historians. Luther research can no longer be satisfied with mere text interpretation, no matter how penetrating and scrupulous. Scholars must now realize that the historical "Luther" and the historical "Reformation" can only be thought of together.

Thanks to the recent, impressively detailed analyses of Luther's early theology done mostly in Zurich and Tübingen, we have a clearer picture of the Reformer's relation to tradition than of his relation to his own contemporaries. Yet much remains to be done. Even without discussing the questions suggested by the particular premises and methods of these theological schools, at least this much should be clear: Luther has wide-ranging and close ties to tradition, which have still not been sufficiently examined. These ties go beyond theology proper. In studying these ties scholars must carefully consider the special conditions which shaped the historical existence of the Reformer—the break with tradition *and* the continuity of tradition, the appeal to the distant past and the posing of problems by the immediate past, the dynamic and the limitation of the Reformation, the delayed development in its complex structure, and what it might be.

3. As for *the other reformers,* we must now go beyond the doubtless pertinent and praiseworthy proof that they differed fundamentally in theology and spirit from the Wittenberg Reformer. Nearly all the other reformers were once humanists. It may be true that humanism, in contrast to the Reformation, had its theological roots in the Middle Ages, and also true that Rome was apparently aware of this fact, since she immediately excommunicated Luther, although she had been content to tolerate the humanist critics up to that point. It is just as unavoidably true, however, that humanists were both the real pioneers and ultimately the real supporters of the Reformation movement.

14

Once having arrived at this conclusion it is high time we consider the even more basic need to understand the specific historical situation as a whole. We need to explore Luther's power of attraction and his lasting influence on the young humanists and thus to analyze the inner coherence of the Reformation movement. In this respect we should clearly realize that it is not only unrealistic but also unreasonable to expect that Luther's followers themselves could have become, as it were, little Luthers, that they should have set aside their own background and put on his. Furthermore, we should free ourselves from the conceptual stereotype of humanism as a type of collective individual. We should also grant that the Protestant humanists represent "an intersection of coherent tendencies."[18] As such, they had an internally coherent "character." We should be on guard against that hermeneutical positivism which believes it has discovered the historical truth about a man's thought once it has analyzed his extant writings. And we should learn to explore the "vital context" or *Sitz im Leben* and not think that the criterion by which we judge a man's theology is obvious from the start.

4. Finally, it seems high time that the *Reformation movement as a whole* once again became an object of research in church history. Let us hope that many historians, who at present may be scared off by the theological monologue, will now resume studies in this area. Through careful observation and analysis of political, socio-economic, intellectual, and spiritual forces we should try to see more clearly the broad outlines and the interplay of events and their profound effects, as earlier generations of historians were able to do. We must attempt to understand the endlessly varied framework of phenomena as they clash and catch fire and as totally different assumptions and experiences, motives and goals are exchanged and unified. Research opportunities lie right before our noses. For example, we have just begun doing precise studies in social history. We still are generally dependent on vague suspicions regarding such elementary questions as the attitude of monks, cathedral chapters, and clergy toward the Reformation. We have not even

18. W. Dilthey, *Gesammelte Schriften* (Leipzig, 1927), 7:135.

15

adequately studied or evaluated the Reformation broadsides and pamphlets, a phenomenon of unique importance and historical significance for the understanding of the background of events. Their gigantic external dimensions would alone merit attention, not to mention their contents and their impact.

A general comment in closing, lest I be misunderstood. I should like to acknowledge the historical justice of the dominant tendencies in Reformation research of the last decades and the enduring and usually basic achievements that they have brought us. I also wish to point out the scholarly thicket in which we are in danger of becoming entangled. Yet my meager suggestions as to how we could perhaps advance a few steps should not be taken as proof of the insignificance of my criticisms. It seems to me that with a refined, mature historicism responsible theologians (leaving historians aside) can no longer evade the task of understanding the historical profundity of the Reformation. We need the spiritual and intellectual energies that the Reformation has to offer. Moreover, the Christian life, the church, and contemporary theology have so many ties to the Reformation that for our own self-knowledge we should always be aware of this relationship, and should continually examine it and test its relevancy for today. We will be lost, however, if we think this can be done without effort at historical understanding.

The German Humanists and the Beginnings of the Reformation

The German Humanists and the
Beginnings of the Reformation

Among the fields of traditional historical scholarship hardly any subject has seen such thorough reappraisal as that intellectual movement of the fifteenth and early sixteenth centuries which for the last century or so has been called humanism. We have learned to understand better the complicated origins of fifteenth-century humanism. We recognize its common bonds with the Middle Ages and scholasticism and its relationship to the Italian Renaissance of the thirteenth and fourteenth centuries. We also know that its essence is only superficially described by such rigid concepts as the love of antiquity. Humanism was rather a gradual discovery of a new feeling for the world and for life, a fresh enthusiasm for the power and freedom of man; and it included a joyous readiness to learn about and to reshape earthly conditions.

We lack a similarly firm knowledge, however, of the end of the humanist movement in the sixteenth century and of its connection with the Reformation. The reformers broke away from their past much more consciously than the humanists did, and it would be temptingly easy to conclude that the movement unleashed by Luther produced a more profound and far-reaching break with the past, at least in external, visible matters, than did humanism. Yet here our understanding of the interconnectedness of the historical conditions surrounding the Reformation movement is often too

19

strongly limited by all kinds of apologetic interests and considerations, or blurred by the gigantic figure of Luther.

In the next few pages we should like to try to describe the context and sources of the humanist reaction to Luther and to his Reformation discovery. We hope in this way to investigate the historical process by which the two movements, humanism and the Reformation, came to be joined together. It is typical that until now this problem has been thoroughly neglected, while the general question of the relationship between humanism and the Reformation has been passionately fought over by traditional research, producing, of course, much more assertion than proof. We shall limit this study to the German humanists since they were the closest to Luther, although an analysis of the humanist movement, at least in the Romance countries, would seem essentially to confirm our conclusions.[1]

We should first attempt to get a rough idea of the humanist movement around 1510. With all due caution regarding typologies it seems to me that we can distinguish two tendencies within the humanist movement at that time. On the one hand, there were the men who were really interested in literary scholarship, like Erasmus, Pirckheimer, or Mutianus Rufus. For such men the humanist heritage, the rebirth of antiquity and especially of languages, was a vocation and a lifelong project. Their ideal, formulated in Mutianus's watchword, *beata tranquillitas,* did not mean merely the external tranquillity required for a quietly contemplative devotion to the *bonae literae* but also included a moral and religious goal: the detachment and freedom from passions attainable, they thought, precisely in scholarship. This detachment made possible for them a reasonable, simple worship, free of all priestly servitude and superstition. These men were accompanied by a huge swarm of enthusiastic but uncreative literati, who exchanged the golden glory of *bonae literae* for chattering and banal versifying and all too easily transformed the moral ideal of *philosophia Christi* into an excuse for immorality.

Alongside this first tradition of humanists, who cultivated ancient

1. Cf. below, n. 47.

studies as ends in themselves or as means of attaining a moral-religious goal, there arose within humanism a new tendency, which, if I see the matter correctly, appeared only after 1500. It aimed at making classical studies even more fruitful by trying to apply the insights won from antiquity to the events and conditions of contemporary everyday life and by seeking not only to understand those conditions but to change them. This new tendency was expressed by the scholarly interest now taken by humanism not only in medicine and natural history, but also in jurisprudence. Here we need not determine to what extent humanism really was able to renew the sciences—current research generally tends to underestimate its success since humanism with its appeal to the authority of the past still stood in the Middle Ages and therefore did not attain an independent basis. The new tendency was also expressed by the entrance of the humanists into politics. After 1500 we can observe everywhere that the positions of power at princely courts and in large imperial cities were being filled by humanistically trained men or that the occupants of these offices were taking remedial steps to obtain humanist training. It is especially noteworthy that at the ecclesiastical courts, where Aleander later complained that the humanist element was particularly strong, even bishops often declared their allegiance to the new movement. Around 1510 one can sense among the humanists a new, strong desire to master the world, a desire not found in this form among the humanists of the fifteenth century, despite the fact that this desire no doubt derived in large measure from the rise of the bourgeoisie, with which the early history of humanism is so closely connected.[2]

Of course, for the early sixteenth century one should not attempt too sharply to distinguish between the two varieties of humanism, which we have tried to describe, even though the distinction is at times clearly evident in a man like Zasius.[3] Often a humanist, like

2. The old contention of E. Troeltsch that humanism differed from the Reformation by being "sociologically completely unproductive" fails to give a faithful image of historical reality; *Historische Zeitschrift* 110 (1913): 534.

3. A. Hartmann, *Die Amerbachkorrespondenz,* vol. 2 (Bochum, 1943), no. 503a.

Konrad Peutinger of Augsburg, developed a profound literary and scholarly erudition alongside his political activity, so that we may speak of an "inner unity of personal culture and public service."[4] We may take as a typical example of this unity the letter of Konstanze Peutinger to her father, who was representing his native town at the Diet of Worms in 1521. Charmingly she describes the longing of his books for the return of their master.[5] Similarly, one finds politicians and scholars together in the sodalities, those groups of humanists which developed at every place of any importance, in every significant imperial city, and at every fair-sized court. In informal fellowship they discussed ideals and those bits of news which flew in letters from town to town, from sodality to sodality, prompted by a nearly inexhaustible loquaciousness, but having little substance.

To round out our picture it is not insignificant that just around 1510 the universities too began to fall more strongly under humanist influence. To be sure, back in the 1480s the great Rudolph Agricola had already gathered a following at Heidelberg. And the most discriminating universities had had for some time the typical humanist lectureships for poetry and for the Greek and Hebrew languages. But around 1510 the new, practical interest began to take effect, and a man like the jurist Zasius found an enthusiastic response among his students at Freiburg.

It is true that the influence of humanism on the life of the universities was almost insignificant, just as in the larger context of the fifteenth and early sixteenth centuries the European universities generally failed to provide the intellectual leadership of their time. Herbert Schöffler has emphasized the fact that the great explorers, Nicholas of Cusa and Copernicus, Columbus, and Gutenberg, all were active in settings untouched by the universities.[6] The faculty of theology in particular was still thoroughly dominated by scholasticism. Yet right in their midst Martin Luther

4. H. Lutz, "Conrad Peutinger" (Diss., Munich, 1953), p. 148.
5. E. König, *Konrad Peutingers Briefwechsel,* Veröffentlichungen der Kommission für Erforschung der Geschichte der Reformation und Gegenreformation, vol. 1, part 1 (Munich, 1923), no. 210.
6. H. Schöffler, *Die Reformation* (Bochum, 1936), pp. 82 f.

now made the most revolutionary of all discoveries, by learning a new way to understand the gospel, the incarnation of God in Jesus Christ. With this discovery he wrenched the whole fabric of the Western world and thereby redirected humanism as well.

Before we turn to the Reformation movement itself, let us establish briefly the extent to which Luther had come in contact with humanism by 1517. It is today generally accepted by scholars that this contact was very superficial. Before 1517 Luther had corresponded with a few humanists: Spalatin, Mutianus, and Scheurl. But in these cases the initiative for the correspondence came from these men, and Luther expressed his sense of inferiority to them more spontaneously and sincerely than was common among the humanists. During his time at Erfurt it seems that he had no serious contact with the group of humanists there. One could even go so far as to assert that Luther *wanted* no such contact. In March of 1517, to be sure, Luther called the prince of the humanists "our Erasmus," but already half a year earlier he had criticized Erasmus's conception of *justitia* [righteousness].[7] On the other hand, the fact that Luther prized the philological research of the humanists and energetically defended the teaching of the ancient languages at Wittenberg is now as well known as his enthusiastic use of the Greek New Testament of Erasmus. As Rückert said, "with striking diligence he brought himself to the heights of humanist learning."[8] Yet for him all of this was only a means to an end. He had absolutely no understanding of the real heart of humanism, its feeling for life and its correspondingly high evaluation of man. Thus regardless of exactly how one understands Luther's reforming discovery—and opinions on this point are certainly most diverse—it cannot in any case be deduced from the intellectual world of humanism. Luther's discovery was more a rejection of that world. One could better call it a monastic discovery.

Because we need some kind of fixed date, we are justified in

7. *WA*, Br 1, nos. 35 and 27.
8. H. Rückert, *Die Stellung der Reformation zur mittelalterlichen Universität* (Stuttgart, 1933), p. 22.

celebrating that day which since 1617 has been viewed as the beginning of the Reformation, the day on which Luther nailed his theses to the castle church in Wittenberg.[9] For our further deliberations, however, we must emphasize that this event, standing at the beginning of a great movement, was a normal action in the framework of late-medieval scholastic university life, and that therefore the Ninety-five Theses have nothing in common with humanist pamphleteering like the *Letters of Obscure Men*.

Yet, as we know, the theses struck an extraordinarily responsive chord. In retrospect Luther later said that they "almost raced through all of Germany in fourteen days."[10] Even if this assertion is tempered somewhat by the relatively small number of reprintings, still the success of this piece of scholastic and scholarly writing is thoroughly remarkable. Unfortunately historians today can trace its impact only in a fragmentary way. As far as we can tell, however, the success of the theses was crucially dependent on the distribution and approval which they enjoyed among the humanist sodalities. We must imagine that they proceeded in triumph, recommended and sent from one humanist group to the next. Christoph Scheurl in Nuremberg, for example, seems to have worked as a regular agent, sending the theses on to Peutinger in January, 1518.[11]

9. Recently H. Volz has demonstrated that the theses were posted not on October 31 but on November 1, 1517; *Deutsches Pfarrerblatt* 57 (1957): 457 f. In other words, for 350 years we have celebrated the festival of the Reformation on the wrong day! Cf. also K. Algermissen in *Catholica* 12 (1958): 75–79.

10. 1541 in "Wider Hans Worst," *WA* 51:540 [*LW* 41:234]. Oecolampadius spoke similarly as early as 1519 in his work, *Canonici indocti Lutherani*. He said that the theses "were distributed with amazing speed throughout Germany and were welcomed with special favor by all of the learned"; E. Staehelin, *Das theologische Lebenswerk Johannes Oekolampads,* Quellen und Forschungen zur Reformationsgeschichte, 21 (Leipzig, 1939), p. 110. The suspicion of J. Luther that the old accounts of the quick spread of the theses really meant the "Sermon on Indulgences and Grace" does not fit with these words of Oecolampadius. For other reasons it is also unconvincing; J. Luther, *Vorbereitung und Verbreitung von Martin Luthers Thesen*, Greifswalder Studien zur Lutherforschung und neuzeitlichen Geistesgeschichte, no. 8 (Berlin, 1933), p. 38. J. Lortz is more cautious: "The Sermon 'displaced' the Theses"; *Die Reformation in Deutschland*, 3rd ed. (Freiburg, 1949), 1:250.

11. F. Freiherr von Soden and J. K. F. Knaake, *Christoph Scheurl's Briefbuch,* vol. 2 (Potsdam, 1872), no. 156. In addition, several persons, including Eck, had already received from Scheurl the "Disputation against

And the theses were immediately reprinted in Leipzig and Basel, and perhaps in Nuremberg,[12] i.e., in centers of the humanist movement.

It is quite obvious that Luther found his most important following in the next months and years among the communities of humanists. This does not of course mean that only they acclaimed him. We know that even his early writings from the years before 1520 were extremely widely distributed and that he was already doubtless the most popular religious writer in Germany.[13] It is, however, not without significance that this general popularity was based almost exclusively on short, edifying treatises. The polemical writings were not especially popular except among the humanists, who repeatedly wrote that they took a special pleasure in them.[14] In those first years there was no real Lutheran movement among the people, and there seem to have been remarkably few pamphlets or preachers from that time that laid claim to Luther's ideas and distributed them farther. For this audience Luther was known not as a party leader but as a pastor.

It was otherwise among the humanists. They were enthusiastically on his side from the time the theses were posted; they declared their unity with him and made his cause a matter of party

---

Scholastic Theology" of September, 1517 (*WA*, Br 1, nos. 46 and 49), and it is possible that they were more widely known than we can tell today. In any event it is clear that Luther was not completely unknown when he attacked indulgences.

12. O. Clemen, *Luthers Werke in Auswahl* (Berlin, 1933), 1:2 f.

13. On this point, cf. H. Dannenbauer, *Luther als religiöser Volksschriftsteller*, Sammlung gemeinverständlicher Vorträge und Schriften, no. 145 (Tübingen, 1930). Even so, the assertion of Scheurl that by November of 1518 Luther was the most famous man in Germany sounds somewhat exaggerated (Soden and Knaake, *Briefbuch*, no. 174). Scheurl was only repeating what he had heard among his humanist friends. The same can probably be said for the remark of Zasius in December, 1519: "Luther is esteemed by all of Switzerland, Constance, Augsburg, and a good part of Italy"; K. Gillers, *Der Briefwechsel des Conradus Mutianus*, Geschichtsquellen der Provinz Sachsen, no. 18 (Halle, 1890), no. 587. Similarly with regard to the numbers in Aleander's well-known report from the Diet at Worms: "Nine-tenths (of the Germans) shout the battlecry, 'Luther!' and for the remaining tenth who do not care about Luther the watchword is 'Death to the Roman court'"; P. Kalkoff, trans., *Die Depeschen des Nuntius Aleander*, 2nd ed. (Halle, 1897), p. 69.

14. Cf. the proof in Dannenbauer, *Luther*, pp. 38 ff. and 31 f.

principle. By their applause and their complementary efforts they drove him forward, carrying his name into town council chambers and into the halls of princes as well. In this way Luther finally became a factor in the calculations of the politicians, although not on any large scale before 1520. The humanists were the one united group of men to stand behind Luther in the first years. However inappropriate their position as representatives of public opinion in Germany, there can be no doubt that it was the humanists who were decisive in dragging the Reformation movement, against Luther's will, out of the obscurity of the humble University of Wittenberg into the light. Luther's cause would not have gone on to victory without the approval of the humanists.

What was their approval like? The most striking feature was how very general and all-inclusive it was. From the great men of the older generation, from Reuchlin, Erasmus, Wimpfeling, Zasius, and Pirckheimer, to the young men, we know of hardly a single humanist who did not at least once in those early years have a friendly word to say about Luther. It was with joy that he was hailed by Mosellanus and Capito, Crotus Rubeanus and Adelmann, Beatus Rhenanus and Amerbach. Bucer and Hutten rapturously swore allegiance to him. Even men who were soon to be his bitter opponents, like Cochlaeus and Fabri, gave him warm approval at first.[15]

No doubt about it, they considered Luther one of their own. They said that explicitly often enough. The young Martin Bucer, in his famous and detailed report of May 1, 1518, regarding Luther's Heidelberg Disputation, wrote to Beatus Rhenanus describing Luther: "They all agree with Erasmus, but one man seemed to stand out, for what he (Erasmus) merely implies, this one (Luther) teaches openly and freely."[16] Hutten asserted that even if the man from Wittenberg were killed a thousand times, a hundred

15. Even Eck was not at first totally inimical. Cf. his letter of 13 October 1518 in H. Ankwicz von Kleehoven, *Johann Cuspinians Briefwechsel*, Veröffentlichungen der Kommission zur Erforschung der Geschichte der Reformation und Gegenreformation, no. 1, part 2 (Munich, 1933), no. 38.
16. A. Horawitz and K. Hartfelder, *Briefwechsel des Beatus Rhenanus* (Leipzig, 1886), no. 75.

new Luthers would arise.[17] Albrecht Dürer picked up this thought in a peculiar way after Luther disappeared in 1521. He suggested that now Erasmus of Rotterdam should take over the position of the man believed dead.[18]

To understand these opinions it is illuminating that Luther was praised for *one* characteristic, and sometimes only one, his sagacity and learning. Just read the enthusiastic reports of Melanchthon or Mosellanus regarding the Leipzig Disputation,[19] or listen to Franz Irenicus as he solemnly declared as early as 1518: "Among all the Germans we wanted to honor Martin Luther with the name of standard bearer on account of the exceptional erudition attained by so great a man."[20] Similarly Bernhard Adelmann of Augsburg in describing the followers of Luther went so far as to equate "learned" with "Lutheran."[21] Beatus Rhenanus exclaimed "I see the world coming to its right mind,"[22] and Johann von Botzheim, canon of Constance and a zealous admirer of Erasmus, praised Luther for finally leading theology into the renewal that the other sciences had enjoyed for some time.[23]

In marked contrast to these reactions from the early period of the humanist sodalities, Oecolampadius noted in 1519 that Luther's exposition of the Ten Commandments "made us feel loftier on account of Christ and holier on account of the gospel. . . . We attribute little, or rather nothing, to ourselves, and much, or rather everything, to God in Christ."[24] Just as exceptional was the statement of Zasius, even after he had broken with the Reformer, that Luther had nonetheless taught him "to follow Christ much more

17. In Aleander; Kalkoff, *Depeschen*, p. 150.
18. F. Leitschuh, *Albrecht Dürer's Tagebuch der Reise in die Niederlande* (Leipzig, 1884), p. 84.
19. *Briefwechsel Melanchthons* 1, Corpus Reformatorum 1, no. 43. J. Schilter, *De libertate ecclesiarum Germaniae* (Jena, 1683), pp. 840 ff.
20. Cited in K. Bauer, *Die Wittenberger Universitätstheologie und die Anfänge der deutschen Reformation* (Tübingen, 1928), p. 62.
21. In Bauer, *Wittenberger Universitätstheologie*, p. 63. See also above, n. 10.
22. Letter to Zwingli, 26 December 1518; *ZW-CR* 7, no. 53. Horawitz and Hartfelder, *Briefwechsel*, no. 83.
23. *WA*, Br 2, no. 264.
24. In the work cited above in n. 10; Staehelin, *Lebenswerk*, p. 109.

truly."[25] Luther's real intentions were thus only rarely recognized by his first humanist adherents. Bucer, in the above-mentioned report from Heidelberg, could only record with surprise the fact that Luther's paradoxical disputation theses denied the free will of man.[26]

Yet Luther did voice certain demands which were closely parallel to those of the humanists, and which explain their sense of solidarity with him. I will select two of the most commonly cited. First of all, there is Luther's rejection of scholasticism. The reformer spoke the inmost thoughts of a humanist with sentences like this one from the "Disputation against Scholastic Theology" [1517]: "All of Aristotle is to theology as darkness is to light,"[27] or this one from a letter to Lang in 1517: "Our theology and that of St. Augustine are advancing very well. . . . Aristotle is gradually declining."[28] The fight of Erasmus and his friends for the simplicity, purity, and reasonableness of Christianity was after all a bitter battle against the life-denying scholastic system with its obscurity and lack of concern for the sources, and against the narrow-mindedness of its contemporary representatives. For example, Mosellanus, in his enthusiastic report on the Leipzig Disputation, wrote that "he (Luther) has hissed the Aristotelian philosophy off the theological stage."[29] And Melanchthon described the same disputation as a fight between primitive Christianity and Aristotle.[30] The humanists reveled in the fact that Luther was leading theology away from abstract speculation and back to life itself.

The second innovation of Luther that especially won the humanists to his side was related to the first. It was the discovery and glorification of Holy Scripture. It is clear that this must have

---

25. Gillers, *Briefwechsel,* no. 587. The same is true of Lazarus Spengler's glorification of Luther's doctrine of justification in 1519. Cf. H. von Schubert, *Lazarus Spengler und die Reformation in Nürnberg,* Quellen und Forschungen zur Reformationsgeschichte, no. 17 (Leipzig, 1934), pp. 189 ff.
26. Cf. the conclusion of J. W. Baum, *Capito und Butzer,* Leben und ausgewählte Schriften der Väter . . . der reformierten Kirche, no. 3 (Elberfeld, 1860), p. 99.
27. Thesis 50. *WA* 1:226 [*LW* 31:12].
28. *WA,* Br 1, no. 41 [*LW* 48:42].
29. Schilter, *De libertate,* p. 843.
30. See above, n. 19.

profoundly inspired the men to whom Erasmus had given the slogan *Ad fontes*. One should recognize, moreover, that Luther was only able to make his scriptural principle understandable, his rejection of appeals to two sources, scripture and tradition, in an age that had been prepared by humanist ideas. Such proposals for reform would have been (and were) unintelligible fifty or a hundred years before Luther.

Both of these ideas of Luther, however, were at certain points decisively different from the similar demands of the humanists. In the case of scholasticism the Reformer was not so upset about the way Aristotle's philosophy obscured true theology as he was about its conversion into a theology of glory [i.e., a theology concerning the essence of God apart from his incarnation]. And in the case of the scriptural principle the slogan *sola scriptura* was equivocal. For the humanists it had an inclusive sense ("not without scripture") while for Luther it was exclusive ("with scripture alone"). For the Reformer the Bible was valuable not on account of its antiquity but because of its message, in which the Bible became "the word for me."

In general one can conclude that the humanists, unlike Luther, stood on the foundations of medieval Catholicism. The old church surely knew that it could tolerate with some indifference the humanist attacks, in contrast to those of Luther. In fact the church had even begun to incorporate the humanist movement inasmuch as her leaders throughout Europe were themselves humanists. We may find a telling symbol of the unity of humanism and Roman Catholicism against Luther in the preface which Erasmus wrote, dedicating his new edition of the New Testament to Leo X. In this dedication Erasmus compared his edition with the mighty structure of St. Peter's Cathedral, the very structure which was to reflect perfectly the earthly power and glory of the Roman church and which at that moment literally broke the unity and glory of that church.

It was a constructive misunderstanding that made the humanists into supporters of Luther, and it is not too much to say that this misconception raised the Reformation from the concern of one man to a revolution in world history. Luther himself had no small part in this misunderstanding. From 1517 on he energetically sought contacts with the humanists. For some time he signed his letters "Eleutherius" [Greek for "free"],[31] and corresponded with Reuchlin and Erasmus.[32] Probably the Reformer was not clearly aware of the gap that divided him from the humanists. This is also true of his relationship with Melanchthon after he arrived in Wittenberg in 1518. There is no doubt that Luther was serious when he occasionally remarked that he should really defer to Melanchthon as John the Baptist did to Christ.[33]

Nonetheless, this unequal alliance, such as it was, could not last forever. Slowly the new ideas became firmer, and Luther attacked and rejected not only parts of the old theology but more and more components of church practice. Slowly too on the other side the representatives of the Roman church fortified and solidified their position and finally separated themselves from Luther. Amid these developments it became increasingly clear to the humanists that the man from Wittenberg was not a simple member of their party and that they would have to transform their current sympathy for him into a firm decision either for or against him.

Strictly speaking, it was only in this situation that humanism revealed its true essence. After 1520 the evangelical movement began to escape from humanism. Luther was now supported by the people and by politicians. Among the polemics of the two great confessions, humanism was unable to establish a third popular rallying cry. The love of antiquity was no longer attractive. To Melanchthon's horror, university youths now simply pushed humanist studies to one side.[34] Almost overnight the new era had lost

---

31. The first time was 31 December 1516; *WA*, Br 1, no. 31. In other words, he did not begin this style only after posting the theses as Bauer (*Wittenberger Universitätstheologie*, p. 133) and others have contended.

32. *WA*, Br 1, nos. 120 and 163.

33. *WA*, Br 2, no. 327. In the same place Luther alludes to the relationship between Elijah and Elisha. Cf. also Luther's remark to the Archbishop of Trier at the Diet of Worms in 1521: "I am only one of the least. Twenty others more learned could take my place." Quoted by Lortz, *Die Reformation in Deutschland*, p. 51.

34. Cf. the interesting examination of this in W. H. Neuser, *Der Ansatz der Theologie Philipp Melanchthons*, Beiträge zur Geschichte und Lehre der Reformierten Kirche, no. 9 (Neukirchen, 1957), p. 34.

30

all use and understanding for itinerant poets and vagabonds. As an independent movement humanism fell apart, and a true humanist tradition survived through the centuries at only a few specially favored places, such as Basel or in the Netherlands.[35] Erasmus's dream of a glorious kingdom of *bonae literae* disappeared. As the humanists now divided themselves between the two great parties, however, they more or less permeated them both with their spirit, and this decisively influenced them for the future. Thus humanism stayed alive, not as a system of organized ideas, but in its intellectual attitude, and was able to pass on much of its essence.

It is our task to outline the beginnings of this development. Let us try to establish the pattern that pervaded this split or division in the humanist movement after 1520.

1. For many humanists it turned out that their religious assumptions were ultimately Catholic. None of them, of course, was as familiar with the theology and life of the Roman church as the monk, Martin Luther. But also for that reason, despite their angry words, none of them rejected that church as fundamentally as he. Thus they proceeded to recant and reject all, or at least some, of their charges against the old church. They now accepted what they had formerly reviled with scorn and disgust, and they now actually became strong or at least moderate Catholics. Indeed for many of them the old church gained new potential, and for some, such as Erasmus, we have the impression that it was only now that they learned to value what the church offered.

2. It seemed to them that as early as Luther's revolutionary writings of 1520, even more so after the disturbances of the fanatics, and definitely with the Peasants' War, the Reformation movement threatened to degenerate into open revolt. In contrast to this apparent threat Christoph Scheurl maintained that "of all men I am the most placid,"[36] and Erasmus in 1519 was already recommending "civil modesty" to Luther.[37] Mutianus declared, "I for

---

35. Cf. W. Kaegi, *Humanistische Kontinuität im konfessionellen Zeitalter*, Schriften der Freunde der Universität Basel, no. 8 (Basel, 1954).
36. Soden and Knaake, *Briefbuch*, no. 214.
37. *WA*, Br 1, no. 183.

one do not love the fanatic stone throwers."[38] And the old church promised more leisure for studies, perhaps even with the assistance of a nice benefice, and the peaceful opportunity to purify Christendom through quietly effective, persistent influence. In this concern these primarily literary and religious humanists were joined by those men who hoped to make ancient studies useful in practice. Their readiness to act often conflicted with their reluctance to overturn the old order of law and justice by force. Thus even the humanists who were jurists and politicians often remained remarkably cool toward Luther.

3. Herbert Schöffler has thrown light on this in a surprising fashion. He pointed out the enormous significance of the "generation gap" for the history of the Reformation movement. When Luther posted his Ninety-five Theses, he was still a young man, barely thirty-four years old. Yet all of his adherents both in Wittenberg and elsewhere were even younger. In contrast, Luther's first Catholic opponents, except for Eck, were all older than the Reformer. During the early years of conflict the Wittenberg faculty, which by and large supported Luther, was in Schöffler's words "probably the youngest body of teachers in the whole history of German universities." On the other hand, the first theological faculties to reject Luther (at the universities of Cologne, Louvain, and Paris) were all superannuated.[39] In the years after 1517 the University of Wittenberg had a constantly growing number of students until the town contained almost as many students as inhabitants. Schöffler contended that it was probably "the most youthful city that ever made a mark for itself in German intellectual history."[40] In contrast, all the other German universities, which, as is well known, were not prepared to join the Reformation, experienced a rapid decline in enrollment, and some of them even had to close down. The Reformation, therefore, appears to have been a rebellious movement of the younger generation against the older.

38. Gillers, *Briefwechsel,* no. 620.
39. Schöffler, *Die Reformation,* pp. 37 f.
40. Ibid., p. 37.

A closer scrutiny of the split within humanism caused by the Reformation confirms Schöffler's observations. Almost all of the humanists who joined Luther were younger than he. And the great men of the older generation—Erasmus, Reuchlin, Zasius, Wimpfeling, Pirckheimer, and Peutinger—all gradually turned away from Luther. Wolfgang Capito, the later reformer of Strasbourg, who was a few years older than Luther, hesitated an extraordinarily long time before siding with Luther. As a result, the men of Wittenberg were still reviling him as a Judas in 1523.[41] One thing should be noted, however: while one can state that the reformers were all young, the converse does not hold, for there were many young humanists who did not join the Reformation.

The explanation of this general phenomenon is not hard to find. It is essential to revolutions that they are made by the young and distrusted by the old, who perhaps are skeptical of new ideas, or who refuse to defer to their youngers, or who simply love tranquillity. In the case of the Reformation there were two additional factors. First of all, some of the important points of contention in the early period provided just the sort of cause for which young people could mount the barricades—freedom from monastic vows and celibacy, from the idea of authority and original sin.[42] Secondly, the particular history of humanism helps to clarify the nature of the division which it underwent. It was men of the older generation who had forged the humanist achievements of freedom and a rebirth of antiquity. In contrast, their students, the younger generation, only had to learn; they had never had to fight seriously. As a result, the ideals of humanism were not as dear to them as to their elders, and they relinquished them more easily. Their teachers, for their part, were not ready to jeopardize their accomplishments in a second revolution.

4. Thus the innovations of the Reformation did not fill the younger humanists with fears about preservation of order. On the contrary, many young people found in Luther's struggle with the

41. P. S. Allen, *Opus epistolarum Des. Erasmi Roterodami,* vol. 5 (Oxford, 1924), no. 1374; cf. no. 1368.
42. Schöffler, *Die Reformation,* p. 39.

old order a reason for finally joining the movement. Luther taught them that criticism of Romanism could have a much more profound basis than humanist ideas and that one could turn from mere criticism to constructive renewal. Zwingli even turned this argument against Luther in one of his works on the Eucharist.[43] It is clear that Luther could speak to that enthusiasm for practical learning which we found as a peculiar characteristic of humanism after 1500. The Reformer could attract these humanists, literary men, scholars, and sometimes even politicians, because he gave new strength to their own conscious or unconscious desires.[44] It seems evident, therefore, that if Luther had appeared fifty years earlier with his demands for the reconstitution of church and world, he would probably have found few supporters since he would have lacked the preparation provided by humanism. It is clear that Luther relied on a dynamic already present in his humanist followers. This is most evident in the fact that the Reformation was most radical in its overthrow of the old traditions wherever former humanists were in control. Just consider the winter of 1521/22, when the fanatics dominated Wittenberg. Luther's friends there, Melanchthon and Justus Jonas, were more or less sympathetic to the prophets. In this sympathy they parted company with the theological ideas of the much more conservative Luther. Similarly, Zwingli in Zurich and the reformers of South Germany and of Switzerland (almost all of whom were originally humanists) forcefully and radically abolished images and the mass. One of the most basic theological differences between Zwingli's Reformation and Luther's was the clear emphasis of the Swiss on the principle of community, in contrast to the stress on office in Wittenberg. To be sure, these differences between Zurich and Wittenberg can be explained in other ways that would depict the South German and Swiss Reformation as city reformations in an old and cultured

43. In his commentary on Micah in 1527, *ZW-CR* 5:721 ff.
44. On the other hand, those young humanists who decided to remain in the old church reflected the same tendency by moving away from the negative reaction of the first polemicists toward an inner reform and toward a Counter-Reformation. Among recent works, cf. especially W. Lipgens, *Kardinal Johannes Gropper,* Reformationsgeschichtliche Studien und Texte, 75 (Aschaffenburg, 1951).

region over against Luther's construction of a university reformation in a newly colonized region. But to explore this theme would go beyond the limits of our present topic. [See "Imperial Cities and the Reformation" below.]

Those humanists who remained Protestants were now more profoundly influenced by Luther than they had been in their initial enthusiasm. They accepted not only his conclusions but also the basic idea that man becomes free for action through faith in the forgiveness of God. In this connection it is worth noticing that between 1518 and 1523 most of them changed their profession, or at least their everyday activity—this in remarkable contrast to Luther himself, who did not change his profession from 1512 to his death in 1546. Generally these former humanists rushed into pastoral and preaching positions. It seems to me that this fact is important for it shows how deep and revolutionary an impression Luther had made. It is of course true that none of his supporters experienced the breakthrough from the old to the new as profoundly as Luther did. Hardly any of the younger or older humanists had Luther's yearning for a gracious God, his consciousness of sin. Who among them therefore could completely grasp the bliss of Luther's discovery that God in Christ becomes our righteousness?! Yet the readiness of these men to renounce their old life-style on account of the gospel and to enter an often dangerous occupation should warn us not to exaggerate the continuity between humanism and the Reformation. For most of the humanists, going over to Luther's side was a real conversion, a recognition of God's majestic authority and a new willingness to serve God obediently.[45]

We have concluded our historical analysis. Let us try to clarify the significance of the conclusions we have reached. First, the ecclesiastical reform movement displays an astonishing situation which, as far as I can see, has never been clearly seen before. Around 1530 the ten or twenty most important intellectual leaders

45. W. Näf, *Vadian und seine Stadt St. Gallen* (St. Gallen, 1957), 2:163, has documented this point beautifully for Vadian. Cf. also the analysis of A. Rich, *Die Anfänge der Theologie Huldrych Zwinglis* (Zurich, 1949), who proves rather too much, in my opinion.

of the movement all had their origins in humanism. The only exceptions were Luther himself, the increasingly marginal figure of Carlstadt, and Nikolaus Amsdorf, who was Luther's colleague, first supporter, dear friend at Wittenberg, and indeed the only man who could really pour Luther's discoveries into the old molds of scholasticism. It seems obvious that the common opinion that humanism had no significance for the Reformation[46] is false when expressed so simplistically. The humanists were the first to accept Luther and to give him a lasting following. It was they who first made his cause into a far-reaching movement. Without them he would have failed as did many before him who had tried to stand up against the old church. One can state this pointedly: No humanism, no Reformation.[47]

The fact that the Reformation was led by humanists was naturally of enormous consequence for subsequent history. Here we can only sketch a few points and must pass over the long-term influence of humanism on the growth of Protestant orthodoxy or on the growth of the Counter-Reformation, as well as the significance of humanism for the history of attempts to reunite the faiths.[48]

It is obvious that the Reformation adopted humanist ideas. Individual reformers no doubt differed among themselves in the extent to which they were bound to the humanist world of thought, but they all differed from Luther in one thing. In a very general sense and without oversimplification it can be said that they all (but not Luther) had at one time celebrated the power of man.

---

46. For example, B. C. Neumann in *Deutsche Vierteljahrschrift für Literaturwissenschaft und Geistesgeschichte* 12 (1934): 166.

47. In passing it should be noted that in the Romance countries it was also humanists who first welcomed Luther. Of course, there the first enthusiasm was, naturally, not so general as in Germany.

48. The fundamental work is R. Stupperich, *Der Humanismus und die Wiedervereinigung der Konfessionen,* Schriften des Vereins für Reformationsgeschichte, 160 (Leipzig, 1936). I cannot go into the question of the connection between the Anabaptist-Spiritualist movements of the Reformation period and humanism. On this subject, cf. R. Kreider, "Anabaptism and Humanism," in *Mennonite Quarterly Review* 26 (1952): 123–41, which does not, however, exhaust the topic.

The new discovery of the mercy of God and of our inability in the face of God did not simply eradicate the heritage of humanism.

Perhaps this conclusion can help explain the apparent fact that all the other reformers of the first generation came to differ with Luther on certain theological questions and that they unconsciously formed a common front against him. On at least two subjects this was clearly the case. First, in the doctrine of justification, despite a fundamental retention and recognition of the *sola gratia* and *sola fide,* there was a regular shift of interest away from justification toward sanctification. It is characteristic that later, during the Majorist controversy,[49] it was none other than Amsdorf who defended the extreme formula that good works were actually harmful for salvation. The second deviation was in the understanding of the Lord's Supper. One could perhaps say that none of Luther's contemporaries, friend or foe, fully grasped his true desire in fighting for the real presence, that is, to confirm the presence of the living Christ as a comfort for us.[50] Perhaps from our viewpoint we could summarize the difference between Luther and the other reformers by emphasizing the fact that they, with their origins in a rather optimistic, orderly, and secure sense of being, could not understand in its profundity the need of Luther the monk for forgiveness and comfort. Nor did the Bible provide for them the comfort which Luther found so momentous and liberating. Of course this answer leaves much unexplained. For at one point

49. Georg Major and Nikolaus Amsdorf were involved in a dispute during the 1550s regarding the necessity of good works for salvation [Ed.].

50. Perhaps the Württemberg reformer Johann Brenz is an exception of sorts. O. Fricke, *Die Christologie des Johann Brenz,* Forschungen zur Geschichte und Lehre des Protestantismus 1/3 (Munich, 1927), has shown that Brenz, who did receive a typical humanist education, nevertheless came very close to Luther theologically. This point is now confirmed by the study of F. Kantzenbach, "Die Bedeutung des Theologen Johannes Brenz für eine Theologie der Anfechtung," in *Das Wort Gottes in Geschichte und Gegenwart* (1957), pp. 160–71. The author points out the meaning of *Anfechtung* (anxiety or temptation) for the theological thought of Brenz. A comprehensive, modern biography of Brenz seems to me to be urgently necessary. It should also examine the neglected question of the connections between the Swabian reformer and late-medieval theology and piety. [Since Moeller wrote these words, Martin Brecht has begun to fill this gap. Ed.]

Luther surely had the chance to become a humanist, and he chose the monastery instead. And the humanists in turn gave up their orderly security and followed him.

This study does not solve the problem of the origins of the Reformation. In a way we are even farther from a solution than before. It is easy to imagine that history could have turned out differently. Luther could have spent his whole life as a little professor who might have occasionally got into trouble with the ecclesiastical authorities but who would hardly have been known outside his university and his order. Similarly, the general excitement at the beginning of the sixteenth century might not have focused on Luther but could have been dispersed into separate movements of social rebellion, pious sectarian withdrawal, and the new paganism of the humanists. In this way the medieval world might have gradually dissolved.[51] It is one of the great puzzles of history that this did not happen and that instead Luther, the great untimely outsider, unleashed a movement, became its focal point, and even largely determined its pattern. It shows us how wrong it would be to think that we have explained a historical movement once we know the ideas of the participants and how perverse it would be to attribute the victory of the Reformation to a misunderstanding.

51. It seems to me that the well-known notion (as in J. Haller, *Die Ursachen der Reformation* [Tübingen, 1917], pp. 30 f.) that Luther's appearance worked like a spark in a powder keg is too superficial and also not justified by the historical context. In opposition to this view, cf. Neumann (above, n. 46), p. 170; in arguing with W. Andreas, Neumann said, "To conclude that 'things could not continue this way' is dangerous reasoning *ex eventu*. Indeed, time and again things have continued in the same way in spite of 'an electric tension'." Cf. also the reflections of K. Holl, *Gesammelte Aufsätze zur Kirchengeschichte,* 7th ed. (Tübingen, 1932), 1:14.

Imperial Cities
and the Reformation

Imperial Cities and the Reformation

INTRODUCTION

The imperial registers drawn up at the Diet of Worms in 1521 list a total of eighty-five cities under the title of "Free and Imperial Cities" (*Frei- und Reichsstätt*).[1] At that time some sixty-five of these cities could be considered directly subject to the empire. The great majority of them, more than fifty, in some way officially recognized the Reformation during the sixteenth century. Over half of the cities became and remained Protestant. Others permitted a Protestant congregation to exist alongside a congregation of the old faith, either from the beginning of the Reformation or in the course of its development. A third group of cities adopted the Reformation, either completely or in part, only to have it later forceably repressed. As far as I can see, of these sixty-five cities only fourteen never officially tolerated a Protestant congregation within their walls during the sixteenth century, although most of these, too, had to deal at times with strong Protestant movements. I know of only five small imperial cities in Swabia and Alsace that remained untouched by the Reformation: Buchau am Federsee,[2] Pfullendorf, Zell am Harmersbach, Rosheim, and Türkheim. But

---

1. A. Wrede, *Reichstagsakten unter Kaiser Karl V* (Gotha, 1896), 2:440 ff.
2. This town does not appear on the imperial registers, however, probably because it was mortgaged in 1521 and became free only three years later, as was the case with Kempten. Cf. K. O. Müller, *Die oberschwäbischen Reichsstädte, ihre Entstehung und ältere Verfassung* (Stuttgart, 1912), p. 329.

41

even in their case the lack of source materials may conceal significant events.

Even from these rough statistics it ought to be apparent that the Reformation penetrated the imperial cities far more deeply than the other estates of the empire. Strangely enough, no one to date has seriously considered these phenomena. Therefore, the attempt to elucidate and interpret these phenomena in a broad and inclusive overview seems especially significant.

In a desire to obtain the most extensive survey possible, we will not restrict ourselves to the imperial cities in the strict legal sense of the word[3] but will encompass those cities which, although not constitutionally subject to the empire directly, yet had at the beginning of the sixteenth century the importance and position of imperial cities. Certain important towns in northern Germany as well as the major towns of German-speaking Switzerland were in this position.

I. The Imperial City of the Late Middle Ages

We must first try to provide ourselves with a picture of the imperial city of the late Middle Ages.

1.

Research on the character of the German city of the Middle Ages, by continuing the studies done by Gierke[1] a century ago, has led to important insights in recent decades. By throwing a strong

3. Moreover, this concept raises some difficult questions of constitutional law that I cannot consider here. It should be kept in mind that the nature and degree of liberties granted to the towns varied. And so of the sixty-five cities mentioned in the text there are several whose direct subordination to the empire in the sixteenth century is contested. The small Alsatian cities are such an example (Cf. J. Adam, *Evangelische Kirchengeschichte der elsässischen Territorien bis zur französischen Revolution* [Strasbourg, 1928], p. 381) as is Friedberg in Hesse. W. Fertsch, "Der Rat der Reichsstadt Friedberg i. d. W. im 16. Jahrhundert" (Diss., Giessen, 1913), pp. 112 ff. The dissertation by J. Sieber, "Zur Geschichte des Reichsmatrikelwesens im ausgehenden Mittelalter" (Diss., Leipzig, 1910), pp. 87 ff., shows that although a territory might be enrolled in the imperial registry, this does not prove that this territory was subject directly to the emperor.

1. O. Gierke, *Das deutsche Genossenschaftsrecht* (Berlin, 1868), 1:300 ff. et passim. In addition, from the older research the famous chapter "Die Stadt" in Max Weber, *Wirtschaft und Gesellschaft. Grundriss der Sozialökonomik* (Tübingen, 1932), especially 3:522 ff., is still important.

light on the communal character of the late medieval town, this research has made better known the unique mentality of the German townspeople before the Reformation.[2]

From the eleventh century onward a great number of urban communities, especially in western and southern Germany, called up ancient ideas of German law and forceably gained their independence from the city lord, whether bishop, monastery, or feudal dynasty. They gained the necessary power for such revolts by forming temporary *conjurationes,* or confederations, which later became more permanent, and by placing themselves under the direct protection of the king and the empire. The confederates agreed among themselves to keep the peace, to be unconditionally loyal, and to come to the aid of one another. In return they gained a share of the privileges won by the confederation and enjoyed the protection which it offered.

Other communities achieved a similar independence by other means, for example through the initiative of the princes.[3] Many of these towns experienced their first full bloom under those friends of cities, the Hohenstaufen. From then on they were able to create their own government in the form of a town council or perhaps a mayor. They could build town walls, introduce their own city seal, and demonstrate their freedom by constructing a town hall. To their number were added the royal towns which were established especially in Swabia and Alsace and were granted similar liberties.

The ruling circle within the cities was at first limited to particular groups of burghers, namely, the rich merchants, the *meliores,* the

2. The works of H. Planitz, "Die deutsche Stadtgemeinde," *Zeitschrift der Savigny-Stiftung für Rechtsgeschichte,* germ. Abt. 64 (1944): 1–85, and *Die deutsche Stadt im Mittelalter* (Cologne and Graz, 1954), are of fundamental importance, although controversial at certain points (see the review by W. Schlesinger in *Historische Zeitschrift* 181 [1956]: 352–57, and that by F. Steinbach in *Zeitschrift der Savigny-Stiftung für Rechtsgeschichte,* germ. Abt. 72 [1955]: 294–99). Heinrich Schmidt's penetrating book, *Die deutschen Städtechroniken als Spiegel des bürgerlichen Selbstverständnisses im Spätmittelalter* (Göttingen, 1958), although occasionally affecting exaggerated precision on certain points, tries to encompass the spiritual and cultural world of the imperial city burgher.

3. Running counter to Planitz, recent research has stressed increasingly that development differed from city to city and from region to region. K. Kroeschell, *Weichbild. Untersuchungen zur Struktur und Entstehung der mittelalterlichen Stadtgemeinde in Westfalen* (Cologne and Graz, 1960).

patriciate. From the time of the Hohenstaufen, however, the non-patrician merchants and artisans banded together in mutual associations, either guilds or corporations. During the fourteenth and fifteenth centuries in the course of the so-called guild struggles, they achieved representation on the city councils, at least in western and southern Germany,[4] and often even succeeded in seizing control of the town.[5]

The burghers were now openly receptive to the communal idea. With annual elections of the councils, which were often extraordinarily large,[6] a considerable part of the citizenry was able to take part directly and actively in the government of the city and to acquire at least some expertise in political matters. In the course of time, the citizens became proud of their dignity and aware of their obligations. Such sentiments deepened and became gradually more common. Each burgher understood that he was part of the whole, sharing responsibility for his part in the welfare of the great organic community, the "collective individual,"[7] to which he was tightly bound by laws and duties.[8]

4. The guild movement was unsuccessful in several places, as, for example, the coastal cities of North Germany. W. Andreas, *Deutschland vor der Reformation*, 6th ed. (Stuttgart, 1959), p. 353.
5. In judging the guild movement we should watch for nuances, as pointed out particularly by E. Maschke, "Verfassung und soziale Kräfte in der deutschen Stadt des späten Mittelalters, vornehmlich in Oberdeutschland," *Vierteljahrsschrift für Sozial- und Wirtschaftsgeschichte* 46 (1959): 289–349, 433–76. He shows that we should speak of a "guild hierarchy" and that merchants who were excluded from the patriciate held the real power in the so-called guild movement rather than the artisans. The special study by E. Meuthen, "Der gesellschaftliche Hintergrund der Aachener Verfassungskämpfe an der Wende vom Mittelalter zur Neuzeit," *Zeitschrift des Aachener Geschichtsvereins* 74/75 (1962/63): 299–392, shows, moreover, that the conventional notion that there are two classes of townsmen is a simplification of reality.
6. Thus in the Reformation period the Small Council had no less than sixty-nine members in Augsburg, in Ulm, seventy-two.
7. W. Bofinger, "Oberdeutschtum und württembergische Reformation" (Diss., Tübingen, 1957). Cf. also note 45 in part III.
8. The death penalty could be given for even relatively petty offenses against the community: for running in the streets and thereby injuring a citizen (Riga), for being dangerously negligent with fire or using false measures (Wismar), for secretly scaling the city wall (Constance) or damaging it (Dortmund), for adulterating wine (Soest), for insulting nobles and lords and thereby endangering the city (Riga), and so on. These and countless other examples can be found in W. Ebel, *Der Bürgereid als Geltungsgrund und Gestaltungsprinzip des deutschen mittelalterlichen Stadtrechts* (Weimar, 1958), pp. 152 ff.

Citizens could see this thoroughgoing membership in the urban community every time a new member had to swear an oath to be received into the citizenry, whether as a burgher's son who had reached majority or as a newly accepted foreigner. In addition, the citizens renewed their oath in times of peril to the city.[9] The town was not, therefore, a purely utilitarian association but was rather the place to which the life of each citizen was bound. Whenever the town was endangered, a burgher felt his very life threatened.[10] The town became for him the embodiment of the empire and the center of his world. It also set the absolute limits of his experience. The chronicler of Constance was sure that the comet which glared in the west meant disaster for Basel, for the chronicler of Cologne it meant Liège, for the chronicler of Lübeck it meant the Rhineland.[11] The burgher considered the law of his own town as God's law. God himself led the town into just wars, and a priest with the consecrated host led the troops.[12]

Natural catastrophes and disastrous fires were God's punishment for the sins of the town, and the citizens sought a remedy by uniting in an oath to forswear sin[13] or by having the whole town undertake a solemn procession of repentance with the relics of the town's patron saint. Whoever put his own advantage ahead of the public interest,[14] provoked disobedience, or incited discord, and

---

9. According to Ebel the city oath was of extraordinary importance for the civic spirit and all of urban life. Indeed, the city oath was originally a mutual oath regularly taken by council and burghers on a designated day each year, the "Oath Day." This custom began in South Germany and Switzerland and soon spread everywhere. The urban community was thereby a *conjuratio reiterata*. The taking of the communal oath by a new citizen is a secondary development. For the formulas of the oath see Ebel, *Der Bürgereid*, pp. 40 ff., 62 ff., 148 ff. In his review of Ebel, Kroeschell emphasizes the difference in this regard between North and South Germany. K. Kroeschell, *Historische Zeitschrift* 193 (1961): 131–34, especially p. 133.

10. H. Schmidt, *Städtechroniken*, p. 98; cf. also the especially graphic formula used in Constance in 1540. See note 56 in part II.

11. Ibid., p. 104.

12. Ibid., pp. 86 ff.

13. Bofinger, "Oberdeutschtum," p. 66; H. Schmidt, *Städtechroniken*, p. 91.

14. H. Schmidt, *Städtechroniken*, pp. 43 ff. The history of the concept of "public interest" needs to be thoroughly studied. In the meanwhile see especially A. Diehl, "Gemeiner Nutzen im Mittelalter," *Zeitschrift für württembergische Landesgeschichte* 1 (1937): 296–315.

thereby disturbed the peace, was brought before the court of God himself. Conspirators against the town were treated like Judas.[15]

Material welfare and eternal salvation were not differentiated and thus the borders between the secular and spiritual areas of life disappeared. We can grasp an essential trait of the late medieval urban community if we characterize it as a "sacred society."

The exceptionally high value placed on the urban community and the exaggeration of its religious function, so strange to our modern way of thinking, has consequences of great importance for the church historian. In such towns the civil community was confused with the religious. In principle, we should not even consider them separately, for they coincide.[16]

Just as the main church composed the center of the civic and religious life of the town,[17] so too all citizens were convinced that every civil institution was directly responsible for spiritual and ecclesiastical matters. When, for example, the Basel City Council in the mid-fifteenth century declared, "that the government of every city is established primarily to augment and support the honor of God and to prohibit all injustice and especially the grossest sins and crimes according to the ordinance of holy Christianity,"[18] this signified above all that for the health of the city, the council, as an organ of the community, must intervene against all opponents of God in the city. In this way it felt called on to control the morality of its citizens. As in other towns, when the Council of Ulm in 1508 banished a blasphemer, it justified its intervention by alleging that God Omnipotent could become irri-

---

15. H. Schmidt, *Städtechroniken,* p. 85, n. 152.

16. For the following, see the works by A. Schultze, "Stadtgemeinde und Kirche im Mittelalter" in *Festgabe für R. Sohm* (Munich, 1914), pp. 103–42, and *Stadtgemeinde und Reformation* (Tübingen, 1918), and the different specialized works which they stimulated, among which the dissertation by H. Kienzle, "Rechtliche Grundlagen und Voraussetzungen der Reformation in Heilbronn" (Diss., Tübingen. Heilbronn, 1921), is especially worth mentioning.

17. See on this subject the beautiful study by A. von Brandt, "Die Ratskirche St. Marien im öffentlichen und bürgerlichen Leben der Stadt [Lübeck]," in *Geist und Politik der lübeckischen Geschichte* (Lübeck, 1954), pp. 83 ff.

18. R. Wackernagel, *Geschichte der Stadt Basel* (Basel, 1916), 2/2:871.

tated and punish not only the guilty one but the council and the entire town.[19]

Such considerations give us a better understanding of the political and ecclesiastical measures taken by the urban councils of the late Middle Ages to control the clergy and to shift many ecclesiastical functions to civic deputies. No doubt the hope of centralizing power, the desire for civic prestige, and other motives could have played a large role, which should not, however, be overestimated. In any case, contrary to what historians have believed until now, these reasons do not suffice to explain the attitude of the councils.

When the council took part in reforming the monasteries, for example by controlling those who administered the finances, when it strove to increase the number of priests,[20] when it concerned itself with charity and with the schools, it was with the idea that the communiy as such, and every individual, ought to provide for the common welfare.

The councils were, moreover, not the only ones to act in this way. Individual citizens, for example, stirred up a broad movement to support preacherships for the parish churches of the towns of Swabia at the beginning of the fifteenth century.[21] Elsewhere even the lower classes of the urban population, the corporations and guilds, were embued with the communal spirit. They united not only to defend their economic interests but also to work for the eternal salvation of their members by controlling morals and justice, by supporting altars and masses for the souls of the dead, and so forth.[22]

---

19. E. Nübling, *Die Reichsstadt Ulm am Ausgange des Mittelalters* (Ulm, 1904–1905), p. 417.

20. The Frankfurt Council busied itself with this with impressive singleness of purpose. Cf. K. Natale, "Das Verhältnis des Clerus zur Stadtgemeinde im spätmittelalterlichen Frankfurt" (Diss., Frankfurt, 1957), pp. 53 ff., 80 ff.

21. J. Rauscher, "Die Prädikaturen in Württemberg vor der Reformation," *Württembergisches Jahrbuch für Statistik und Landeskunde* 2 (1908): 152–211; E. Lengwiler, "Die vorreformatorischen Praedikaturen der deutschen Schweiz" (Diss., Freiburg i. U., 1955). In 1495–96 this custom also spread to Lübeck; cf. M. E. Schlichting, "Religiöse und gesellschaftliche Anschauungen in den Hansestädten des späten Mittelalters" (Diss., Berlin, 1935).

22. Planitz, *Deutsche Stadt,* pp. 291 ff.

Now if the citizens and the magistrates were so convinced that their community was responsible for the salvation of its members, they were almost bound to come into conflict with the ecclesiastical institutions whose juridical structure was foreign to them. Of course, in those imperial cities where a bishop resided, the opposition against him was as old as the liberty of the city itself.[23] For a burgher who could hardly tolerate residents who were not full members of the civic community, it was hardly endurable that the eternal salvation of the city should be dependent on a source of authority outside the city walls, especially when in the late Middle Ages that source for well-known reasons was losing the respect and the confidence of the populace and no longer seemed to satisfy the needs of the city. From this point to the thought that the community ought to regulate itself was no more than a short step.[24]

The governments of the cities began systematically taking over the distribution of ecclesiastical prebends. At the end of the Middle Ages, they achieved a real monopoly of patronage[25] and made the church into a sort of "private church" (*ecclesia propria*) reserved for the urban community.[26] Behind such moves often stood the hope of thereby controlling the quality of the clergy and of assuring the continuation of divine services and the administration of the sacraments in times of general crisis for the church. In short, they strove to guarantee the priestly means of salvation for the city.

These considerations very probably played a decisive role in the community demands that priests submit to the jurisdiction of the

23. According to B. Dauch (*Die Bischofsstadt als Residenz der geistlichen Fürsten* [Berlin, 1913]) as a result of conflicts with citizens nearly all the German bishops of the late Middle Ages resided temporarily or permanently outside their city. See F. Merzbacher, *Die Bischofsstadt* (Cologne, 1961), pp. 26 ff., 45.

24. For that which follows see A. Störmann, *Die städtischen Gravamina gegen den Klerus am Ausgang des Mittelalters und in der Reformationszeit* (Münster, 1916).

25. Such was the case at Esslingen. Cf. K. Müller, "Die Esslinger Pfarrkirche im Mittelalter," *Württembergische Vierteljahrsheft für Landesgeschichte*, n.s. 16 (1907): 272.

26. K. Neumann, "Das geistige und religiöse Leben Lübecks am Ausgang des Mittelalters," *Zeitschrift des Vereins für lübeckische Geschichte* 21 (1921/23): 129.

city,[27] pay taxes,[28] and take the oath of citizenship,[29] demands which already appeared in part in the fourteenth century. As has recently been convincingly proved especially for the case of Strasbourg, the same context explains the attempts of magistrates of independent episcopal cities to exercise a decisive influence over the building of cathedral churches in the territory of the city.[30] Since the town of the Middle Ages conceived of itself as a sacred society, its government necessarily assumed various spiritual tasks. It may be possible to see here the seeds of those tendencies destined ultimately to oppose the hierarchical church.[31] Yet they certainly wanted to remain Catholic and members of the church, both in faith as well as in ordinary life. Indeed, if our interpretation is correct, the above-mentioned infringements of the burghers on the ecclesiastical domain had no other goal than stimulating the spiritual life.[32] Nonetheless, it was without scruples that the town decided to settle disciplinary and administrative questions and to assume the responsibility of carefully preparing the way to eternal salvation without submitting to the church hierarchy. By exaggerating a bit, one could assert that the German town of the late Middle Ages tended to view itself as a miniature *corpus christianum*.[33]

2.

As early as the fifteenth century the urban organism began to show signs of weakening. For many reasons the inner and outer situation of the towns changed after the "guild struggles."

27. Störmann, *Gravamina*, pp. 178 ff.

28. Ibid., pp. 160 ff.

29. F. Heer, "Augsburger Bürgertum im Aufstieg Augsburgs zur Weltstadt," in *Augusta, 955–1955* (Augsburg, 1955), p. 116.

30. Cf. P. Wiek, "Das Strassburger Münster. Untersuchung über die Mitwirkung des Stadtbürgertums am Bau bischöflicher Kathedralkirchen im Spätmittelalter," *Zeitschrift für die Geschichte des Oberrheins,* n.s. 68 (1959): 40–113. This instructive essay shows in detail how the city government gradually took over construction of the cathedral, effectively controlling the direction of work, without any apparent political motive for this action, at least in the early period.

31. Bofinger, "Oberdeutschtum," p. 62.

32. Schultze, *Stadtgemeinde und Reformation,* p. 27.

33. I do not intend by this sentence to go as far as Bofinger, who claims that the urban community in the late Middle Ages considered itself to be a *church*.

From the fifteenth century onward conflicts with the princes became incessant. Earlier the urban confederation had been able to triumph over the feudal system because of its strict juridical organization[34] and had attracted both commerce and prosperity. Yet, when the individual princely states began to group and centralize their power, cities discovered that their political power was becoming too weak to guarantee their economic interests, which depended on freedom of commerce. Thus many formerly free cities whose independence had not been legally or politically secure enough fell under "foreign" domination. No wonder that the princes appeared to the burgher of the fifteenth century as the real enemy of the city, and the opposition between authoritarian lordship and the community, as it became more intense, was felt by every burgher.[35]

Since they had to defend their existence against neighboring lords, the towns were forced in the course of the fifteenth century to strengthen the authoritarian aspects of their own government. Many an imperial city seized control of its surrounding territory. Some like Nuremberg, Ulm, and many Swiss towns, considerably expanded their wealth and power this way, even though they never attained truly Italian proportions.[36] On the other hand, from the end of the fifteenth century on, the artisans fell into severe difficulties in selling their products, which forced the town council to take increasingly energetic and wide-ranging measures. It was especially necessary to supervise closely the guilds, to regulate the

34. There is a good sketch of the general development in the work by K. Jordan, "Herrschaft und Genossenschaft im deutschen Mittelalter," *Geschichte in Wissenschaft und Unterricht* 12 (1961): 104–15.

35. Legal historians repeatedly warn against exaggerating this opposition (see in particular K. S. Bader, *Der deutsche Südwesten in seiner territorialstaatlichen Entwicklung* [Stuttgart, 1950], p. 92). According to O. Brunner ("Stadt und Bürgertum in der europäischen Geschichte," *Geschichte in Wissenschaft und Unterricht* 4 [1953]: 525–37), the urban community is even a special form of feudal structure. In the context of our study, however, we must remember that a burgher in an imperial city saw lordship and community as mutually exclusive (the book by H. Schmidt, *Städtechroniken,* offers a number of convincing examples).

36. F. Rörig, *Die europäische Stadt und die Kultur des Bürgertums im Mittelalter* (Göttingen, 1955), p. 113; H. Dannenbauer, *Die Entstehung des Territoriums der Reichsstadt Nürnberg* (Stuttgart, 1928); O. Hohenstatt, *Die Entwicklung des Territoriums der Reichsstadt Ulm im 13. und 14. Jahrhundert* (Stuttgart, 1911).

market, to smooth out conflicts of competition, and so forth.[37]

Another innovation led to the same result. The imperial cities slowly acquired the right of taking part in the imperial diets. After 1486 they were regularly invited, and after 1489 they formed their own separate chamber.[38] Thus the constitutional situation in the empire became clearer. Significantly for the history of the Reformation, the imperial cities were from that point on fundamentally different from territorial cities even in their external relations. Their horizon was enlarged. Even in the smallest of them, the council developed a sort of foreign policy. Yet from the beginning the imperial cities at the diet found themselves in a weak position. Their needs and interests were so diverse and their democratic governments so subject to conflicting advice that they could rarely unite in a common policy. No wonder that they were not taken seriously and that their reliability was doubted.[39] Therefore, from this additional point of view, it seemed advisable to strengthen the city government. The bureaucracy had to be extended; the importance of the city secretaries rose, for example, since they took part in the administration of the city as full-time professionals appointed for life. Beginning in the early sixteenth century many of them were learned in the law.[40] Thus the city government was no longer dependent on the community in the full sense of the word. In addition, the kinds of tasks assigned to the elected officials changed during the fifteenth century. The business of the city became ever more complex and demanded increased experience as well as time and money. Sometimes month-long ambassadorial trips were necessary for the town councillors, who by law received no salary.

Dating from this period a candidate's hereditary descent (*Ab-*

---

37. See particularly E. Naujoks, *Obrigkeitsgedanke, Zunftverfassung und Reformation. Studien zur Geschichte von Ulm, Esslingen und Schwäbisch Gmünd* (Stuttgart, 1958), p. 11.
38. F. Hartung, *Deutsche Verfassungsgeschichte vom 15. Jahrhundert bis zur Gegenwart*, 6th ed. (Stuttgart, 1959), p. 38.
39. References in the work by Naujoks, *Obrigkeitsgedanke*, pp. 26 ff.
40. G. Burger, *Die südwestdeutschen Stadtschreiber im Mittelalter* (Böblingen, 1960).

kömmlichkeit),[41] whether from the patriciate or commons, played a large role in his evaluation for a position on the council or in the administration. One should of course recognize that the patricians and rich merchants had always exercised more real influence than the artisans in civil government, even where they had earlier been officially excluded from power. But they now often regained control of important offices. Frequently the achievements of the guild struggles degenerated back into mere theory. In reality, the large council and communal assembly[42] were often no longer in actual control of affairs. There were not a few towns where the guilds retained a majority in the council but where for decades the mayors were all patricians.[43] It is, therefore, quite proper to speak in this regard of an "oligarchical tendency"[44] in the evolution of cities toward the end of the fifteenth century. The relationship between the magistrates and the community changed. The council of the city of Ulm, for example, already considered itself as the "ruler" and the members of the citizenry as "subjects,"[45] and after 1500 it addressed the burghers in formal language instead of familiarly as before.[46]

Moreover, in the late fifteenth and early sixteenth centuries the upper classes of the imperial cities formed the elite of the whole empire,[47] and the intellectual life of Germany reached a truly European level for the first time. With wealth the cultural demands of the burghers were rising.[48] They had learned to read and write

41. This term of Max Weber's is used by Maschke. He shows with impressive examples how the upper classes penetrated municipal government in the fifteenth century. Maschke, "Verfassung und soziale Kräfte," pp. 351 ff., 467 ff.
42. In the large cities of German Switzerland, this assembly never met again. L. von Muralt, "Stadtgemeinde und Reformation in der Schweiz," *Revue d'Histoire Suisse* 10 (1930): 356.
43. Examples in Maschke, "Verfassung und soziale Kräfte," pp. 313 ff.
44. Naujoks, *Obrigkeitsgedanke*, p. 19.
45. Ibid., p. 15.
46. Ibid., p. 29.
47. See especially the article by W. Andreas, "Die Kulturbedeutung der deutschen Reichsstadt zu Ausgang des Mittelalters," *Deutsche Vierteljahrsschrift für Literaturwissenschaft und Geistesgeschichte* 6 (1928): 62–113, and the chapter on the city in his book, *Deutschland vor der Reformation*, pp. 343 ff.
48. The comparison with the Italian cities is instructive. See H. Kellenbenz, "Der italienische Grosskaufmann und die Renaissance," *Vierteljahrsschrift für Sozial- und Wirtschaftsgeschichte* 45 (1958): 145–67.

like clerics. Humanism blossomed in their midst. Above all, they bought the books of the great printers, who had their workshops in imperial cities like Augsburg, Nuremberg, Basel, and Strasbourg. They gave painters their greatest commissions.

Nevertheless, one can sense behind all this brilliance an inner unrest. Especially in towns where trade with distant regions flourished and where some merchants amassed enormous fortunes, as in the Hanseatic cities and in Augsburg, the gap between the wealthy and the poor grew, and real hatred of the rich emerged. Around 1510 trouble exploded in many places. Not only were economic demands advanced, but the ancient ideals of community were again held up against the tendency toward lordship. The people demanded participation in their own government and also, for example, the restriction of membership on the council to a single representative from any one family.[49]

In general then, by 1520 we can feel the beginnings of a change in the way these urban communities viewed themselves. Everyone was still conscious and proud of being a citizen of his city. Yet the cohesion of the members of the community was relaxing as their sense of responsibility for the common welfare weakened. And similarly the old conception of the solidarity of the citizens before God was no longer deeply felt. This phenomenon is most visible among the humanists. They no longer considered the town to have any connection with eternal salvation.[50] Instead, they praised it by reaching back to that ancient idea of the perfect republic which guaranteed peace on earth.[51] Jakob Wimpfeling translated "public interest" with *respublica*.[52]

49. Cf. the work by K. Kaser, *Politische und soziale Bewegungen im deutschen Bürgertum zu Beginn des 16. Jahrhunderts* (Stuttgart, 1899).
50. Nevertheless, one can still find this sentiment expressed by the humanist Jakob Wimpfeling in certain passages of his *Germania*.
51. Bofinger, "Oberdeutschtum," pp. 53 ff. The comprehensive and enthusiastic description made of Ulm's constitution by the Dominican Felix Fabri in his *Tractatus de civitate Ulmensi*, ed. Veesenmeyer (Stuttgart, 1899), is particularly well known, especially pp. 59 ff. and 126 ff. We should mention here the poems of the humanists praising the cities (see J. Neff, *Eobanus Hessus' Noriberga illustrata und andere Städtegedichte* [Berlin, 1896], as well as Erasmus to Wimpfeling, 1514, on the perfection of the government of Strasbourg. P. S. Allen, ed., *Opus epistolarum Desiderii Erasmi Roterodami* [Oxford, 1910], 2:18 f.).
52. E. W. Kohls, *Die Schule bei Martin Bucer in ihrem Verhältnis zu Kirche und Obrigkeit* (Heidelberg, 1963), pp. 123 ff.

II. The Introduction of the Reformation
into the Imperial Cities

Considering just the numerical data, we were able to see how deeply the Reformation took root in the imperial cities. We came to the same conclusion by noting that the free cities were the first communities officially to embrace the Reformation.[1] We will now try to give a general view of the introduction of the Reformation into the imperial cities and to determine precisely why this kind of territory was more favorable than others. Yet from the outset we should recognize that in the sixteenth century, more than in almost any other period, each imperial city had its own peculiar destiny, regardless of all general tendencies and deeper interconnections.

1.

The first admirers of Luther in the cities as elsewhere were the *humanists*. The most detached from the medieval world, with the clearest recognition of the limits of the church, they were the most disposed to accept new ideas. They opened the first breach for the Reformation. Of course, a good number of the humanists of the imperial cities supported Luther only briefly. Scheurl and Pirck-heimer of Nuremberg, Konrad Peutinger (who had offered Luther hospitality after the hearing with Cajetan), Rychard of Ulm, Hummelberg of Ravensburg, and many others abandoned Luther rather quickly.[2]

The Reformation preaching found another breach provided by the social tensions of which we spoke earlier. As early as the disorders following the year 1510, a newly rising estate of journeymen, trade workers,[3] and even guilds which were excluded from

1. One should always remember that the "introduction of the Reformation" is a vague concept that must be exactly defined for each case (on this subject, cf. the remarks of G. Pfeiffer, "Die Einführung der Reformation in Nürnberg," *Blätter für deutsche Landesgeschichte* 89 [1952]: 112–33, especially p. 112). Still, one can properly call Zurich the first Protestant state. It was followed quickly by Nuremberg, Strasbourg, Memmingen, and Constance in South Germany and by Magdeburg in the North.
2. On this subject see the preceding essay by Bernd Moeller, "The German Humanists and the Beginnings of the Reformation," pp. 19–38. [Ed.]
3. Cf. H. Preuss, *Die Entwicklung des deutschen Städtewesens* (Leipzig, 1906), 1:106 ff.

city government, showed their dislike of the rich and powerful[4] in explosions of hatred against the prosperous church[5] and in savage riots against the Jews, who were held responsible for the economic decline.[6] Similar unrest reappeared in the early period of the Reformation. With Luther's appearance on the scene, these antagonisms reached an acute phase, and in the cities, as among the peasants, social and ecclesiastical demands came together. In many places citizens demanded simultaneously from their council a Protestant preacher, suppression of tax payments to the church, and greater participation in city government.[7] Or they insisted on concessions from the council for the Protestant movement to balance off their consent to church taxation.[8]

In 1525, the year of the Peasants' War, townsmen and peasants[9] made alliances in several places at the center of the uprising, at Heilbronn, Schweinfurt, Regensburg, and Nordhausen. At Rothenburg on the Tauber and, under the leadership of Müntzer, at Mühl-

4. For example in Schweinfurt. Cf. F. Stein, *Geschichte der Reichsstadt Schweinfurt* (Schweinfurt, 1900), 2:97 ff.

5. Especially in Goslar in 1518. Cf. U. Hölscher, *Die Geschichte der Reformation in Goslar* (Hannover, 1902), p. 14. This episode is not mentioned in K. Kaser, *Politische und soziale Bewegungen im deutschen Bürgertum zu Beginn des 16. Jahrhunderts* (Stuttgart, 1899).

6. Especially at Regensburg in 1518–19. Cf. R. Straus, *Die Judengemeinde Regensburg im ausgehenden Mittelalter* (Regensburg, 1932); the collection of source materials announced when this work first appeared was finally published in 1960. A description of the pogrom is also to be found in the work by L. Theobald, *Die Reformationsgeschichte der Reichsstadt Regensburg,* 2 vols. (Munich, 1936), vol. 1. Cf. also P. Herde, "Gestaltung und Krisis des christlich-jüdischen Verhältnisses in Regensburg am Ende des Mittelalters," *Zeitschrift für bayerische Landesgeschichte* 22 (1959): 359–95.

7. For example, in the Alsatian city Mulhouse, which from 1515 on was part of the Swiss Confederation. Cf. J. Adam, *Evangelische Kirchengeschichte der elsässischen Territorien bis zur französischen Revolution* (Strasbourg, 1928), pp. 554 f.

8. This happened in the Hanseatic cities. Cf. W. Jannasch, *Reformationsgeschichte Lübecks vom Petersablass bis zum Augsburger Reichstag* (Lübeck, 1958), p. 275, et passim; L. von Winterfeld, *Geschichte der freien und Hansestadt Dortmund* (Dortmund, 1934), p. 135; J. Schildhauer, *Soziale, politische und religiöse Auseinandersetzungen in den Hansestädten Stralsund, Rostock und Wismar im ersten Drittel des 16. Jahrhunderts* (Weimar, 1959), pp. 121 ff.

9. However, Mistele has shown that the rebels in Heilbronn came from all social classes and that their goal was not so much a social revolution as obtaining political influence. K. H. Mistele, *Die Bevölkerung der Reichsstadt Heilbronn im Spätmittelalter* (Heilbronn, 1962).

hausen in Thuringia, genuine brotherhoods of Protestant-minded communities and peasant masses led to city support for the Peasants' Revolt.[10] Apparently, even the Twelve Articles of the peasants were penned by a citizen of an imperial city.[11]

Still, in most cases the Protestant ministers turned against the rebellion[12] and, characteristically, the urban Reformation party was often able to keep its distance from the peasants. A good example is Schwäbisch Gmünd, where the committee, which had been formed by citizens revolting against their council and which now ruled the town, nevertheless maintained a stony reserve toward the attempts of the peasants at an alliance.[13] On the whole, it is significant that the Peasants' War remained a peasants' war.[14]

However, the year 1525 was crucial to the Reformation in several cities. This was particularly the case for the localities directly hit by the Peasants' War. Sometimes the reaction which followed the peasants' defeat forcefully accelerated the Reformation.[15] But we also have clear evidence that in many places in Franconia and

10. P. Schattenmann, *Die Einführung der Reformation in der ehemaligen Reichsstadt Rothenburg ob der Tauber* (Munich, 1928), pp. 61 ff.

11. The author was almost certainly the furrier Lotzer from Memmingen. Cf. G. Franz, "Die Entstehung der zwölf Artikel der deutschen Bauernschaft," *Archiv für Reformationsgeschichte* 36 (1939): 193–213.

12. K. Kaser, *Politische und soziale Bewegungen*, pp. 216 f., pulls together the meager evidence relating to the social agitation of Protestant preachers in cities.

13. E. Wagner, "Die Reichsstadt Schwäbisch Gmünd in den Jahren 1523–1576," *Württembergische Vierteljahreshefte für Landesgeschichte* 2 (1879): 86; E. Naujoks, *Obrigkeitsgedanke, Zunftverfassung und Reformation. Studien zur Geschichte von Ulm, Esslingen und Schwäbisch Gmünd* (Stuttgart, 1958), p. 63. At Heilbronn the rebels, in the very first of their demands, referred to their civic oath and made assurances that they were not lacking in that obedience which the oath required. M. von Rauch, *Urkundenbuch der Stadt Heilbronn* (Stuttgart, 1922), vol. 4, no. 2794; Kaser, *Politische und soziale Bewegungen*, pp. 239 ff., gives other examples of the reserve displayed by townsmen in Upper Germany toward the peasants.

14. And not only because of the political cleverness of the councils. Cf. Preuss, *Die Entwicklung des deutschen Städtewesens*, 1:116.

15. For example, in Alsatian towns like Wissembourg and Sélestat (Adam, *Elsässischen Territorien*, pp. 421 ff.), and in Kaufbeuren (cf. K. Alt, *Reformation und Gegenreformation in der freien Reichsstadt Kaufbeuren* [Munich, 1932], p. 42), but especially in Schwäbisch Gmünd, where the council, forcefully supported by the Swabian League, was able to reestablish its authority and that of the Roman church; Gmünd succeeded in maintaining this position throughout the following years, although drastic measures were necessary. Cf. Naujoks, *Obrigkeitsgedanke*, pp. 60 ff., 71, 96 ff.

Thuringia the townsmen, disturbed by the disorders and disenchanted with the Reformation, were prompted to new loyalty to the Roman church.[16]

In this connection we should also mention the reform movement in Cologne in 1525. In this city, the "German Rome," Luther's writings were burned as early as 1520 with the consent of the council, and in following years all Protestant movements were repressed by joint action of the council, the university, and the clergy. In 1525, however, a strong opposition group formed which, among other things, would have "gladly imposed Lutheranism and demanded freedom."[17] At first they were able to gain ground against the council, which was intimidated by the widespread unrest. But this group lost its courage when the peasants were defeated. Thus Cologne remained the only large imperial city and the only free episcopal city that was incontestably Catholic despite recurring Protestant stirrings among the people.[18]

In many cities, therefore, the connection of demands for Reformation with desires for social and economic reform more likely retarded than accelerated the victory of the Reformation. The fact that Luther could still win on such a broad front indicates that we cannot limit ourselves in this study to the exterior signs of discontent among the city inhabitants.[19]

16. Thus in Rothenburg in May, just after the defeat of the peasants, two hundred burghers submitted a petition demanding the reestablishment of the mass (Schattenmann, *Die Einführung der Reformation*, p. 63); cf. also the referendum on the Reformation at Bopfingen, which (according to Irtenkauf's article in the *Rieser Nachrichten* of 14 June 1962) took place as early as 1525 and not in 1526 (as O. Clemen, "Zur Reformationsgeschichte von Bopfingen," *Blätter für württembergische Kirchengeschichte*, n.s. 33 [1929]: 159–63, had thought), and which resulted in defeat for the Protestant preachers; these are two almost unique events in the history of the Reformation in the imperial cities.

17. K. Höhlbaum, *Das Buch Weinsberg* (Leipzig, 1887), 1:43.

18. L. Ennen, *Geschichte der Stadt Coeln* (Cologne, 1875), pp. 225 ff.

19. F. Lau, in his important article, "Der Bauernkrieg und das angebliche Ende der lutherischen Reformation als spontane Volksbewegung," *Luther-Jahrbuch* 26 (1952): 109–34, takes off from the history of the Reformation in the North German towns and forcefully rejects the widespread opinion that, with the year of the Peasants' War, the Reformation movement lost its popular momentum and became an affair solely for the magistrates. In what follows we shall see that the conclusions of Lau are completely applicable to the imperial cities of South Germany.

2.

The decisive impulse that explains the enthusiasm of the imperial cities for the Reformation came obviously from much more profound sentiments. For example in Speyer in 1525, a committee of townsmen demanded that the payment of taxes to the church be abolished because the pious foundations had been "fraudulently" established, while it was now known "by godly truth that they were neither useful to the dead nor to the living."[20] Again in 1528, some Hamburg artisans demanded the punishment of Catholic clergymen, "who have led us poor people into error with their indulgences and their holy purgatory."[21]

The profound transformation caused by the Reformation can be seen in an indirect but much more tangible fashion in the iconoclasm which it produced in a number of cities. To appreciate this phenomenon properly, we must recognize the evidence for the most ardent medieval cults of piety in the German imperial cities just before the Reformation. At Schwäbisch Hall the entire city paraded along the banks of the Kocher in 1520 when the river was at flood and was endangering the saltsprings. They carried the sacrament in a "splendid procession" to appease God's wrath toward the city.[22] Yet within two years Brenz was preaching there.

The history of the Reformation at Regensburg is an even more impressive example of the collision of two ages.[23] In 1519, after the expulsion of the Jews, the town planned to build a Christian chapel where the synagogue had stood. During the demolition work, a most gratifying miracle occurred, and from then on the

20. J. M. König, *Reformationsgeschichte der Stadt Speyer, oder das evangelische Speyer, nebst andern sich darauf beziehenden, merkwürdigen Nachrichten in Noten und einem Anhange, von 1439–1834* (Speyer, 1834), pp. 20 ff.

21. Quoted by K. Beckey, *Die Reformation in Hamburg* (Hamburg, 1929), p. 107.

22. G. Rücklin-Teuscher, *Religiöses Volksleben des ausgehenden Mittelalters in den Reichsstädten Hall und Heilbronn* (Berlin, 1933), p. 122. Profound spiritual differences existed, however, among the imperial cities, as is evident in a comparison with Strasbourg. During an epidemic in 1518, the council of that city urged the citizens to have recourse to the prayers of the preachers instead of to medicine, instead of to a procession of supplication. F. Braun, *Orthodoxie und Pietismus in Memmingen* (Munich, 1935), p. 195.

23. For the following, cf. Theobald, *Regensburg*, 1:33 ff.

construction of the little church became a great communal effort, almost the self-realization of the town. Citizens made enormous donations, and the whole town took part in the work. One day three hundred women, maids, and little girls even helped by carrying stones [in procession], led by a lighted church lantern and by the church banner with the picture of the Virgin. The building was quickly finished and a pilgrimage began at once to the Beautiful Maria, a movement so extensive that those of the Middle Ages could hardly rival it. The council, doubtless desirous of profiting from such a favorable situation, supported the enterprise as best they could. Thus in 1520 no less than 118,961 plaques had been sold to pilgrims, and in 1521 no less than 209 miracles were recorded. In 1522, however, one hundred to one hundred fifty of the townspeople could be considered Lutheran; the same year, the city printer, besides the official reports on the miracles of the Beautiful Maria, published no fewer than eight of Luther's writings, even though Luther in his *Address to the Christian Nobility of the German Nation* had attacked the Regensburg pilgrimage.[24] One year later calm had returned; there was no more need of plaques; pilgrims came no more. In 1524 at least some image breaking erupted but it did not get very far since the council took severe countermeasures.[25] In 1542 the city became Protestant;[26] the famous image of the Beautiful Maria was shattered, and the church received a thoroughly profane name, *Neupfarrkirche* (Church of the New Parish).[27]

24. *WA* 6:447, line 19. A list of works printed at Regensburg in 1522 may be found in the book by K. Schottenloher, *Das Regensburger Buchgewerbe im 15. und 16. Jahrhundert* (Mainz, 1920), pp. 181 ff.

25. Theobald, *Regensburg*, 1:131.

26. The problem of knowing exactly when this town became completely Protestant in the sixteenth century provoked a violent controversy between J. Sydow ("Die Konfessionen in Regensburg zwischen Reformation und westfälischem Frieden," *Zeitschrift für bayerische Landesgeschichte* 23 [1960]: 473–91) and M. Simon ("Beiträge zum Verhältnis der Konfessionen in der Reichsstadt Regensburg," *Zeitschrift für bayerische Kirchengeschichte* 33 [1964]: 1–33).

27. Theobald, *Regensburg*, 2:17, 21. The inhabitants of Weissenburg in Bavaria in 1519 tried unsuccessfully to organize a productive pilgrimage to the chapel they built in place of the synagogue. Competition from Regensburg was doubtless too strong. K. Ried, *Die Durchführung der Reformation in der ehemaligen freien Reichsstadt Weissenburg i. B.* (Freising, 1915), pp. 7 ff.

"The image breakers were also the image donors." This sentence by Hermann Heimpel,[28] which is certainly true for Regensburg,[29] describes exactly how men's spirits were transformed by the Reformation. Those who donated an image did not merely venerate that image; those who broke an image did not merely hate it. Both the donor and the breaker of images were concerned with eternal salvation. In this respect iconoclasm is the most convincing symbol of the profound influence of Protestant preaching.[30] Needless to say, even considering the spiritual agitation of the Reformation, it was possible to give the problem of images a less extreme and, generally, more logical solution than iconoclasm.[31]

The Reformation, apparently, shook the townsmen to their depths, and in the last analysis this explains why Luther found such broad, general support in all of the cities. If we exclude the humanists, we can say that the urban Protestant movement in the first half of the sixteenth century had its basis exclusively among the people.[32] The conclusion of Franz Lau is valid for all of

28. H. Heimpel, "Das Wesen des deutschen Spätmittelalters," in *Der Mensch in seiner Gegenwart. Sieben historische Essais* (Göttingen, 1954), p. 134.
29. Of course, one can doubt whether the image donors and the image breakers in Regensburg were actually the same persons. More detailed research would probably allow us to discover some social differences. But this would not change the general view of the phenomenon. Within a few years the great mass of citizens was swept over to a conception of eternal salvation diametrically opposed to their previous convictions.
30. Although the book by Schildhauer (see note 8 above) is valuable in many respects, it does not consider the connections between these events. The author starts with "the viewpoint of historical materialism . . . and (sees) in religious controversies only an aspect of the ever-increasing class conflict, only a transposition of socio-economic and political struggles to a different level" (p. vii). In this way he binds history with fetters of his dogma and actually grasps only one aspect, without comprehending all of the fullness, profundity, and strangeness of past events.
31. On this subject, cf. H. von Campenhausen, "Die Bilderfrage in der Reformation," *Zeitschrift für Kirchengeschichte* 68 (1957): 96–128.
32. As early as 1523, the Council of Ulm determined that the ideas of Luther had "taken root and grown in the common man." Naujoks, *Obrigkeitsgedanke*, p. 57. Zwingli too observed that, "The common man follows the gospel although his superiors want nothing of it" (*ZW-CR* 3:446, lines 13 ff. [*Wer Ursach gebe*]). In towns that did not become Protestant until the religious Peace of Augsburg, it was the town council that often took the initiative, as in Colmar (Adam, *Elsässischen Territorien*, p. 469) and perhaps in Aachen (H. F. Macco, *Die reformatorischen Bewegungen während des 16. Jahrhunderts in der Reichsstadt Aachen* [Leipzig, 1900], p. 27, et passim). But even here we have evidence of the lively participation of the populace. R. Reuter, *Der Kampf um die Reichsstandschaft der Städte auf dem Reichstag 1582* (Munich, 1919), p. 21.

Germany: "The Reformation was never the work of a town council."[33] Only in a couple of the imperial cities did the council pick up the impulse from the people, at the start or after a short hesitation, and then lead the Reformation quickly and directly to victory. The best-known example of this is Nuremberg, while other cities such as Strasbourg, Constance, Memmingen, and, in northern Germany, Magdeburg, could also be mentioned in this regard.

For the most part, however, the magistrates were anything but the motive force behind the Reformation. They were more often a brake. Let us try to determine the reasons for their attitude. First of all, in considering the ideas of the Middle Ages, we should realize that the councillors felt personally responsible for keeping the peace within the city. If there were suddenly two churches, city unity and the very existence of the city itself was at issue. That is why the Überlingen City Council admonished the community in 1525 to guard itself against the new teachings, "in order that in our city there be no disunion, no discord, no dissension among us as in other communities. Rather we should always live united in peace, in the future as we have up to now. We should therefore remain together, faithfully united in lives, honor, and goods. We should watch carefully to guard ourselves from the poisonous seeds of the new doctrine (which the Lutherans call evangelical) that it does not take root among us."[34]

With the Reformation the whole sacred order, the salvation of the city itself, seemed threatened. So the magistrates exerted themselves almost convulsively to strengthen the ties binding the townsmen to the ceremonies of the old church. For example, the population could be bound by oath to the Catholic ceremonies and teachings.[35] In Schwäbisch Gmünd the rosary was made the sign of membership in the city, and not only were the citizens obliged to

33. Lau, "Der Bauernkrieg," p. 119.
34. Quoted in the work by L. Muchow, "Zur Geschichte Ueberlingens im Bauernkriege," *Schriften des Vereins für Geschichte des Bodensees und seiner Umgebung* 18 (1889): 56.
35. As early as 1527 in Fribourg in western Switzerland. Cf. L. Waeber, "La réaction du gouvernement de Fribourg au début de la réforme," *Revue d'Histoire Ecclésiastique Suisse* 53 (1959): 119 ff.

carry one at all times like identification papers, but the councillors had to keep one in hand during all council meetings.[36] It is highly characteristic that often, especially in later years, the magistrates attempted to force the townsmen to receive the Roman Catholic sacraments. Canon law already stipulated that heretics and excommunicates could not be buried in sacred ground.[37] But the Offenburg Council, to take an example, went clearly beyond this when, plainly worried by Protestant leanings among the populace, it declared in its 1560/61 church ordinance: "Whenever one or more persons have sworn obedience to this our Christian ordinance and yet willfully and wantonly presume to take the sacraments elsewhere (!) and thus separate themselves in this life from our community, this person or persons shall be buried at that same place when they die, and shall be separated and excluded from our cemetery here."[38] This is a totally medieval conception: the sacramental community was the city community.[39]

In explaining the caution of many city governments with regard to the Reformation, we must no doubt take social factors into account. We observed above that the patricians and merchants in many imperial cities held the real position of leadership, either traditionally or only recently, and in accordance with or in spite of the constitution. In many cases, therefore, the natural opposition of the aristocrat to the passions of the multitude and the general conservatism of the rich and privileged held back the revolution, especially since the old church reserved very pleasant rewards for nobility and wealth, like entry into economically comfortable positions and into offices guaranteeing salvation. Thus one observes a general antipathy to the Reformation especially among the patri-

36. Naujoks, *Obrigkeitsgedanke*, p. 102.
37. This had been the rule ever since the Fourth Lateran Council in 1215. Cf. *Corpus juris canonici*, ed. E. Friedberg (Leipzig, 1879–1881), 2:887.
38. Quoted by E. Batzer, "Neues über die Reformation in den Städten Gengenbach und Offenburg," *Zeitschrift für die Geschichte des Oberrheins*, n.s. 39 (1926): 82.
39. A proclamation from Schwäbisch Gmünd provides another especially striking example of the connection in urban thinking between the idea of the peace of the city and the idea of eternal salvation. E. Wagner, "Die Reichsstadt Schwäbisch Gmünd in den Jahren 1531–1545," *Württembergische Vierteljahrshefte für Landesgeschichte* 7 (1884): 14.

cians. In many places they emigrated from cities turning Protestant;[40] in others they remained as a small but powerful and, if
possible, malicious Catholic minority.

It is absolutely clear, therefore, that in those cities where
artisans had a large share of the government, the Reformation was
accepted more quickly than in those led by patricians.[41] In this
respect too, the great exception is Nuremberg, which had a strong
patrician government. But in most of the cities the Protestant
townsmen resolutely pushed these hindrances aside. It is important
to recognize that the Reformation was introduced almost everywhere according to the forms prescribed by the city constitution,
and that it had its foundation in the city's communal mentality. In
this respect, there were hardly any exceptions and only few differences among the free cities of the German language area, although they strongly differed otherwise in regional characteristics,
in social and economic situations, and in their constitutions. Obviously, the urban communal idea was still deeply anchored and
fully alive in the mind of burghers at the beginning of the sixteenth
century, in spite of all that had tended to weaken it in the preceding
period.

Ordinarily, the first step made by the partisans of reformation
was to call for Protestant preaching, demanding that the council
call a Lutheran preacher or that it confirm the one who was al-

40. For example, at Memmingen and at Basel. Cf. F. Dobel, *Memmingen
im Reformationszeitalter nach handschriftlichen und gleichzeitigen Quellen*
(Augsburg, 1877), 3:33; H. Escher, "Die Glaubensparteien in der Eidgenossenschaft und ihre Beziehungen zum Ausland, 1527–1531" (Diss.,
Zurich, 1882), p. 35.

41. This was noticed earlier by G. L. von Maurer, *Geschichte der Städte-
verfassung in Deutschland* (Erlangen, 1871), 4:122. Naujoks (*Obrigkeitsgedanke*) has made this relationship clear by comparing the history of the
Reformation in Ulm and in Esslingen. Constance provides a curious example of the opposite. For several reasons the patricians there were the
leaders of the Protestant movement. This is certainly a unique case in the
history of the Reformation. The most vigorous opponents of the Reformation came from members of the guild of fishers, the lowest social class
among the guilds. B. Moeller, *Johannes Zwick und die Reformation in
Konstanz* (Gütersloh, 1961), p. 103. Yet the fishers in the neighboring city
of Schaffhausen were among the most avid proponents of the Reformation.
Cf. J. Wipf, *Reformationsgeschichte der Stadt und Landschaft Schaffhausen*
(Zurich, 1929), p. 199. It goes without saying that social tensions were at
work.

ready present in the city.[42] Often the supplicants declared themselves personally prepared to undertake the support of the preacher.[43] In many places Protestant townsmen united in a community oath,[44] and often, as in Strasbourg in 1524, they emphasized their demands with the formula of the community: "We in common citizenship will sacrifice our body and blood for the word of God."[45]

The introduction of the Reformation, therefore, occurred usually, if not always, with the direct participation of the community. Often the council organized a vote in the guilds[46] or in a communal assembly, which almost always[47] resulted in an overpowering victory for the Protestant party.[48] In several places the council

42. At Regensburg and Strasbourg in 1523: Theobald, *Regensburg*, 1:126; Bucer, *DS* 1:291 ff. At Esslingen, Sélestat, and Schwäbisch Gmünd in 1524: T. Keim, *Reformationsblätter der Stadt Esslingen* (Esslingen, 1860), p. 16; Adam, *Elsässischen Territorien*, p. 418; Wagner, "Die Reichsstadt Schwäbisch Gmünd in den Jahren 1523–1576," p. 83. At Heilbronn in 1525: M. Duncker, "Zwei Aktenstücke zur Reformationsgeschichte Heilbronns," *Zeitschrift für Kirchengeschichte* 25 (1904): 309. At Giengen and Rottweil in 1529: Andler, "Die Reformation in Giengen an der Brenz," *Blätter für württembergische Kirchengeschichte*, n.s. 1 (1897): 97; J. Speh, "Beiträge zur Reformationsgeschichte des oberen Neckargebietes" (Diss., Tübingen, 1920), p. 28.

43. At Sélestat, Heilbronn, Giengen, Rottweil, Strasbourg, as in the preceding footnote. At Augsburg in 1526: F. Roth, *Augsburgs Reformationsgeschichte*, 2nd ed. (Munich, 1901–1911), 1:296.

44. At Schwäbisch Gmünd in 1525: Wagner, "Die Reichsstadt Schwäbisch Gmünd in den Jahren 1523–1576," p. 83. At Leutkirch in 1546: H. Hermelink, *Geschichte der evangelischen Kirche in Württemberg von der Reformation bis zur Gegenwart* (Stuttgart and Tübingen, 1949), p. 55.

45. J. Adam, *Evangelische Kirchengeschichte der Stadt Strassburg* (Strasbourg, 1922), p. 80. Similarly at Hamburg in 1526: Beckey, *Die Reformation in Hamburg*, p. 51. And in 1536: Ibid., p. 195. At Goslar in 1528: Hölscher, *Goslar*, pp. 27 ff. At Heilbronn in 1531: Rauch, *Heilbronn*, vol. 4, no. 3399, at the end. At Ravensburg in 1546: K. O. Müller, "Aktenstücke zur Geschichte der Reformation in Ravensburg," *Reformationsgeschichtliche Studien und Texte* 32 (1914): 44. For the wording of the oath, cf. W. Ebel, *Der Bürgereid als Geltungsgrund und Gestaltungsprinzip des deutschen mittelalterlichen Stadtrechts* (Weimar, 1958), pp. 146 ff.

46. Following the advice given by Zwingli in 1528 in his well-known letter to Blarer: *ZW-CR* 9, no. 720, p. 457, lines 26 ff.

47. See the exceptions noted above, note 16 of this part.

48. Similar voting took place throughout Upper Germany. At Constance in 1528 (Moeller, *Johannes Zwick*, p. 103); at Strasbourg and Biberach in 1529 (J. W. Baum, *Capito und Butzer* [Elberfeld, 1860], p. 449; G. Luz, *Beiträge zur Geschichte der ehemaligen Reichsstadt Biberach* [1876], pp. 128 ff.); at Memmingen in 1529–30 (Dobel, *Memmingen*, 2:70; 4:22); at Ulm and Weissenburg in Bavaria in 1530 (Hermelink, *Württemberg*, p. 50;

and the community swore a common oath in which each burgher pledged, as in 1528 at Goslar: "If the council and the above-named city is ever in distress and adversity on account of the abolition of the mass or other ceremonies, or on account of the Holy Gospel which is now preached and taught as it ought to be in all its purity and its clarity, I promise allegiance and place my life and my goods in the service of our noble council and in the service of the city of Goslar, so long as I shall be a citizen and inhabitant. So help me God and his gospel."[49]

One can sense the seriousness with which the Protestant parties struggled to win their cities to the Reformation. But ultimately this passionate activity of the Protestant townsmen stemmed from the conception which the medieval city had of itself. It was necessary to conserve at any price the peace of the city. This argument is emphasized both in the petitions of the burghers and in the Reformation decrees of the councils. In contrast to the Middle Ages, everyone was now convinced that the peace could only be maintained or reestablished if the word of God, and it alone, were preached, and this threw into question the traditionally valid ecclesiastical constitution.

As early as July 1523 the city of Mühlhausen in Alsace declared that it wished to place itself under the word of God, "so that Christian brotherly love and unity may be planted among us."[50] And Goslar adopted the Reformation in 1528 to prevent "all discord and disunity in the common citizenry."[51] Such statements

---

Ried, *Weissenburg i. B.*, p. 49); at Heilbronn and Esslingen in 1531 (Hermelink, *Württemberg*, pp. 49, 52). The opposition votes came mostly from the patricians.

49. Hölscher, *Goslar*, p. 32. In the background one can detect a certain reserve of the council with regard to the Protestant movement.

50. Quoted by Adam, *Elsässischen Territorien*, p. 553. Similarly, the Zurich Council in its decree of 17 November 1523, concerning the Reformation, urged the populace to read the Bible in order that "true knowledge and real unity as well as the improvement of our morals may be learned from the word of God." K. B. Hundeshagen, *Beiträge zur Kirchenverfassungs-geschichte und Kirchenpolitik* (Wiesbaden, 1864), 1:199. This particular association of ideas, the acceptance of the word of God and the unity of the townspeople, is found often, even in church ordinances not dealing with free cities.

51. Quoted by Hölscher, *Goslar*, p. 31.

were based on the burghers' resolute conviction, medieval if you wish, that the truth was one and indivisible and that one's attitude toward it determined life and death. If that was true, the task was clear both for the townsmen and for the magistrates, who saw themselves as communal representatives. The town must declare itself against falsity and for truth, against damnation and for eternal happiness. At Constance the council argued this way against the cathedral chapter: "Since there is one God, one faith, one baptism, and since it is necessary above all to maintain peace and unity, it is befitting to an honorable council to encourage all who live inside the walls of the city, whether clergy or laity, to maintain peace and unity."[52]

Such a declaration of the whole city was necessary since God wanted to be honored and wanted his will to be done. If the Catholic abuses were not eliminated, then the whole community was threatened by God's wrath. They thought of this in concrete terms no different from those of the Catholic period. When the vineyards froze at Reutlingen in September 1548, general grumbling arose among the townspeople. Some maintained that the calamity was God's punishment because the city had denied God's word by accepting the Interim, and they sought to annul it.[53] Even a man like Zwingli was convinced that God had "saved Zurich only because it had obeyed the word of God without shirking."[54]

The conviction that the whole urban community stood as a

---

52. M. Krebs, "Die Protokolle des Konstanzer Domkapitels," *Zeitschrift für die Geschichte des Oberrheins*, 106 (1958), 6. Beiheft, no. 8816.

53. J. G. Votteler, *Versuch der Reformationsgeschichte der Stadt Reutlingen* (Reutlingen, 1813), p. 70.

54. *ZW-CR* 9, no. 606 (To Ulm in 1527). The Basel Reformation ordinance of 1 April 1529 was supposed to "increase the honor of God and to implant peaceful and Christian behavior." P. Roth, *Aktensammlung zur Geschichte der Basler Reformation in den Jahren 1519 bis Anfang 1534* (Basel, 1937), vol. 3, no. 473. Similarly, the new church ordinance of Nördlingen in 1538 was to provide for "the salvation and well-being of the whole community." E. Sehling, *Die evangelischen Kirchenordnungen des 16. Jahrhunderts* (Leipzig, 1902–), 12/2:307. Similar thoughts were not even foreign to Luther. Cf. for example his letter of 1529 to the people of Memmingen, who, he thought, had done away with the Lord's Supper: "Beware . . . of a great anger against your city, since among you Christ's word and institutions are considered worthless" (*WA*, Br 5, no. 1422).

unit before God also was obviously bound to influence the internal politics of the city after the introduction of the Reformation. Once the community had decided, by a majority vote if possible, and had moved over to the Reformation, the whole city had to abide by this decision; for "whoever wants to rise above the law would fight with God himself and would cause the ruin of bodies and souls by disturbing the peace of the community."[55] The burghers were so tied together with interwoven bonds "like the limbs of one body, citizens of the same town, and inhabitants of the same home,"[56] that no "discord in the civil union"[57] could be tolerated. Nonetheless, in most Protestant cities, as in Zurich,[58] the Catholics were tolerated as long as they remained quiet. But, for example, the report came from Heilbronn that stubborn Catholics there could be deprived of citizenship,[59] which also happened to Protestants in Catholic towns.[60]

This idea that the city was fully responsible before God seems to have determined the attack of councils on the Catholic institu-

55. These were the words of Brunswick's church ordinance composed by Bugenhagen in 1528. Sehling, *Die evangelischen Kirchenordnungen* (Göttingen, 1955), 6/1, 1:350.

56. The Constance Council used this argument during the plague of 1540 to urge the burghers to piety and unity. Moeller, *Johannes Zwick*, p. 234.

57. In Constance: Moeller, *Johannes Zwick*, p. 84, n. 34. In that footnote one may also find other examples showing that this idea was widespread. Luther said the same thing in his Commentary on Psalm 82, written in 1530. *WA* 31/1:209, lines 15 ff. [*LW* 13:62 f.]. A land with two faiths was not governable. But for him considerations of political expedience were more decisive than the concept of the urban community. There is a different tone with Zwingli, as for example in his lovely letter of consolation to the mayor and Council of Memmingen in 1530: "Above all things, dear lords and brothers, see to it that you are harmoniously of one mind. Granted such unity, no town, no matter how small, is without honor" (*ZW-CR* 11, no. 1114).

58. A. Farner, *Die Lehre von Kirche und Staat bei Zwingli* (Tübingen, 1930), p. 88.

59. Anon., "Die Reformation der Reichsstadt Heilbronn," *Historisch-politische Blätter* 61 (1868): 528. Opponents of the Reformation also had to emigrate from Strasbourg. F. Wendel, *L'Eglise de Strasbourg. Sa constitution et son organization, 1532–1535* (Paris, 1942), p. 175.

60. This occurred in Rottweil from 1546 on, later at Weilderstadt and at Cologne. F. Thudichum, *Geschichte der Reichsstadt Rottweil und des Kaiserlichen Hofgerichts daselbst*, Tübinger Studien für Schwäbische und Deutsche Rechtsgeschichte (Tübingen, 1911), 2/8:48; F. Fritz, *Ulmische Kirchengeschichte vom Interim bis zum dreissigjährigen Krieg* (Stuttgart, 1934), p. 119; Ennen, *Geschichte der Stadt Coeln*, p. 756.

tions in their city. This explains, first of all, the demands that the clergy marry, pay taxes, and acquire the rights of the city, but also the measures taken against convents and pious foundations or even against bishops and cathedral chapters, when the occasion arose. In exactly the same way they justified such improvements as the reorganization of benefices, of schools, and of the control of morals.[61] Of course, these spiritual motives could blend easily with purely political considerations. Yet in all of these actions, the town government could feel in harmony with the ideas and institutions of the late Middle Ages.[62] "Fundamentally, they required nothing new; they limited themselves to increasing their former demands."[63] This statement still seems to be true.

3.

Our description of the external events that marked the transfer of the imperial cities to the Reformation should have already shown that Luther's movement met a situation that was peculiar in two respects. First, it seems that nowhere else were there communities in which Protestant preaching could so readily find an audience. Only in the cities was there such a dynamic union of ruling authority and subjects. It would not have occurred to a single prince to ask his subjects if they wished to introduce the Reformation;[64] similarly in a territorial city the Reformation could only develop if the territorial lord permitted it. Nowhere else was

61. B. Moeller, "Die Kirche in den evangelischen freien Städten Oberdeutschlands im Zeitalter der Reformation," *Zeitschrift für die Geschichte des Oberrheins* 112 (1964): 67–82.

62. A. Schultze, in his book, *Stadtgemeinde und Reformation* (Tübingen, 1918), was the first to demonstrate the relationship between actions taken during the age of the Reformation and those of the late Middle Ages. Since his time, his conclusions have continued to be examined in detail by local historians, who have confirmed them. Cf. for the example of Heilbronn: H. Kienzle, "Rechtliche Grundlagen und Voraussetzungen der Reformation in Heilbronn" (Diss., Tübingen. Heilbronn, 1921), p. 48.

63. J. Lindenberg, *Stadt und Kirche im spätmittelalterlichen Hildesheim* (Hildesheim, 1963), p. 132.

64. The imperial cities themselves were often not gentle with their own territories. With regard to the countryside, the council of an imperial city acted like a territorial prince. On this subject, cf. the useful work by H. Schmolz, "Herrschaft und Dorf im Gebiet der Reichsstadt Ulm," *Ulm und Oberschwaben* 36 (1962): 179–207. This is probably why the villages, and more especially the subject towns, showed less enthusiasm for the Reformation than the populace of the imperial city to which they were subject, as, for example, in Geislingen, a town dependent on Ulm. Fritz, *Ulmische*

the success of the Reformation so little influenced by repression or forceful imposition. Moreover, at least at first, the Reformation gave the imperial cities a new awareness of their original communal foundations. It stimulated a new and vital participation of citizens in communal affairs.[65] Such participation occasionally provoked constitutional changes toward a more democratic government,[66] changes that were sometimes even permanent.[67]

On the other hand, we have seen how strongly the imperial cities experienced their transition to the Reformation as a community, as a city. This means, however, that the Protestant movement in the cities had to confront as nowhere else a special world of thought, aware of its own value, and based on a closed, medieval social order, on which strict discipline had made its mark. The Reformation found this world stimulating but also ran into natural resistances that forced it to explain itself, to accept some compromises, and even to protest.

We will try in the following pages to depict with more detail this inner and doctrinal history of the Reformation in the imperial cities.

III. THE THEOLOGY OF THE REFORMATION IN THE FREE CITIES

We have not yet answered the following question: Why was the preaching of the Reformation successful in the imperial cities, and why was it able to renew a social order several centuries old?

Kirchengeschichte, pp. 51 ff., 137 ff. E. W. Zeeden made the same observation in "Grundlagen und Wege der Konfessionsbildung in Deutschland im Zeitalter der Glaubenskämpfe," *Historische Zeitschrift* 185 (1958): 267, n. 1.

65. This is especially noticeable in the cities of North Germany. Cf. Lau, "Der Bauernkrieg," passim. However, Naujoks has discovered these same side effects of the Reformation in Ulm and in Esslingen.

66. On this subject see especially the article by L. von Muralt, "Stadtgemeinde und Reformation in der Schweiz," *Revue d'Histoire Suisse* 10 (1930): 349–84, which proves this for Bern and Basel. One might also think of the admittedly short period of Wullenwever in Lübeck. For the other Baltic towns, cf. also Schildhauer, *Auseinandersetzungen in den Hansestädten*, pp. 117 ff. For Göttingen, cf. G. Erdmann, *Geschichte der Kirchenreformation in der Stadt Göttingen* (Göttingen, 1888), p. 30; as well as Lau, "Der Bauernkrieg," p. 125.

67. Especially in Hamburg. Cf. H. Mauersberg, *Wirtschafts- und Sozialgeschichte zentraleuropäischer Städte in neuerer Zeit* (Göttingen, 1960), p. 110.

After what we have seen, we cannot content ourselves with explanations involving only the open-mindedness of the townspeople or the social discontent in the cities. Both may have eased the way for the Reformation, but the decisive impulse obviously came from the message itself. We may then pose the question: Why was the Reformation able both to interest and satisfy the townspeople, and why was it the Reformation, among all the other possibilities, that took over and then elevated the late-medieval town to a higher level? What were the points of contact between the theology of the Reformation and the way that a burgher understood his role in an imperial city of the sixteenth century?

It is obvious that these questions have no simple answer. We can give only a cautious and provisional answer without expecting to grasp completely the depth of the historical event. On the one hand, to answer these questions we will have to rely more on suspicion and conjecture, since there are no direct sources. And it is particularly the nature of spiritual revolutions, and even more so with revolutions of piety, that they cannot be really explained. Although our question is more appropriate and profound than any other open to the historian, still it ultimately does not go beyond the surface of events. For the victory of the Reformation was more than the result of theological reflections.

On the other hand, our question is surely not foreign to the subject. There never was a period of German history more interested in theological questions or in which knowledge of theology for its own sake was so widespread among men of all estates and professions as in the first years of the Reformation. Even if the Reformation history of the imperial cities did not provide many direct examples of this, the gigantic mass of theological and devotional books printed and sold before 1525 would supply all necessary proof.[1] It is thoroughly characteristic of the Reformation that it owed its success to laymen, ready to accept in large measure the ideas propagated by a few theologians. This was true even though the clergy, in the cities at least, held

---

1. H. Dannenbauer evaluates a few of them impressively in *Luther als religiöser Volksschriftsteller* (Tübingen, 1930).

back and did not support the Protestant movement. In the minds of those clergy who did not feel deeply attached to the Catholic church, the worry that they were not prepared to meet such new and unaccustomed demands probably often conquered the temptations raised, for example, by the abolition of celibacy.[2]

1.

Now this is precisely the observation that should guide us. Luther taught that only through faith could one receive justification, the proper relationship to and before God. There is no path from the natural man to God. We do not receive salvation through our own moral efforts, by "good works," or by being integrated in a metaphysically based order, say, by belonging to a special class of people. Thus all "works righteousness" is meaningless. But if it is meaningless, and this is particularly important for our study, the medieval division of Christendom into clergy and laity is also meaningless. The subordination of some people to others no longer had any reason for being. The "first wall of the Romanists," the notion that the temporal power had no rights over the spiritual authority, was knocked down.[3] More importantly, before God all Christians were fundamentally of the same estate. And in addition all were "truly of the spiritual estate."[4] The priest was only an "official" called by the congregation to proclaim the word.[5]

These considerations yield two kinds of answers to our question. First, in this formulation Luther gave the existence of the city an entirely new and more profound significance; the fundamental law of the community by which all members were equal in principle and enjoyed the same rights was from then on anchored in

2. Among the materials relating to the imperial cities, the reports from Ulm, for example, are very instructive. When the Reformation was introduced there, it was accepted by five priests out of thirty-five in the city and by twenty-two out of sixty-seven in the country: J. Endriss, *Das Ulmer Reformationsjahr 1531* (Ulm, 1931), pp. 29, 32. One can deduce similar proportions for Constance. If the situation was different in the Swiss cities of the 1520s, we may suspect that the persuasive powers of Zwingli were playing a large role.

3. *WA* 6:407 ff. (*An den christlichen Adel*) [*LW* 44:127 ff.].

4. Ibid., p. 407, lines 13 f. [*LW* 44:127].

5. Ibid., p. 408, lines 13 ff. [*LW* 44:129].

theology. In the ancient struggle between the city and the church, or legally speaking between the corporation and the institution, Luther supported the former against the latter.[6] The integration into the urban community of ecclesiastical persons and institutions was now theologically legitimate.

Yet this was nothing but the reverse side of the much more essential discovery of Luther's, which brought a "genuine Copernican revolution in thought."[7] Secular life itself was now freed of all the inferiority which had been attached to it during the Middle Ages. God himself was its origin and goal. And so Luther declared the exercise of every single calling to be equally a good work before God, as long as it was done in faith. As with the princes,[8] so especially in the towns, this discovery was to have a profound impact since the urban communities had already thought for a long time that the exercise of any profession had moral value in that it was the fulfillment of a function in service to the people. Luther now gave these spiritual tendencies which were derived from this basic principle a more profound justification by showing that the Bible itself sanctified worldly callings and that the magisterial office was a special work of God. Luther placed these activities, like all natural actions, eating or marrying for example, on the same level before God.[9] He opened to the civil magistracy the ancient areas reserved for the church, like supervision of morals[10] and public instruction.[11] In particular, he assigned the right of choosing pastors to the congregation and the civil authorities,[12] and he justified this infringement of the domain of the church with an image that spoke directly to the urban mentality:

6. Cf. A. Schultze, *Stadtgemeinde und Reformation* (Tübingen, 1918), passim.

7. The expression of H. Liermann, "Untersuchung zum Sakralrecht," *Zeitschrift der Savigny-Stiftung für Rechtsgeschichte,* kan. Abt. 30 (1941):322.

8. For the reaction of Frederick the Wise see Luther, *WA* 30/2:109, lines 16 ff. (*Vom Kriege wider den Türken*) [*LW* 46:163].

9. *WA* 11:254, lines 37 ff.; 257, lines 21 f. (*Von weltlicher Obrigkeit*) [*LW* 45:95, 97].

10. *WA* 6:255 ff.; 261 f. (*Von den guten Werken*) [*LW* 44:87 ff., 95 ff.].

11. *WA* 15:27 ff. (*An die Ratsherren*) [*LW* 45:347 ff.].

12. K. Holl, "Luther und das landesherrliche Kirchenregiment," *Zeitschrift für Theologie und Kirche* 21 (1911), Ergänzungsheft 1, p. 356.

Would it not be unnatural behavior, if a fire is raging through the town, for someone to stand back quietly and let it burn more and more wherever it would, only because he does not have the powers of mayor? . . . Is not every burgher here obliged to sound the alarm and call the others?[13]

Luther did not conceive of the state in the modern sense, as an institution, but as a personal union between superiors and inferiors;[14] and in his time this was more applicable to an urban setting than to the princely territories.

In a real sense, however, the discoveries of Luther undoubtedly transformed the old idea. For him the communal relationship was not the central idea but only one of second rank. We recall that the town of the late Middle Ages thought of the individual primarily as a member of the community. The town even considered itself as a kind of intermediary through which the individual found his salvation. The individual shared in the collective salvation of the whole town by becoming a professional and moral part of the community. Luther rejected this kind of thinking. For him the Christian, as far as salvation was concerned, stood alone before God. One could not reach God by membership in a town or by an oath of citizenship. Instead, a twofold personal requirement was set: baptism and faith.

With this conclusion the ancient and simple identification of the parish with the town became impossible. The church, as a community of the faithful, was essentially invisible. Only faith could perceive its unity and its concrete reality. "In his thought the parish no longer clearly separated itself from the civil community."[15] The citizen was no longer permitted to believe that his good behavior was sufficient to lead him to salvation. Only as a believer could man establish a truly moral relationship with his community, obeying God's commandments, serving his neighbor, and practicing his vocation responsibly.

Fidelity to the community as a "good work" bringing salvation

13. *WA* 6:413, lines 33 ff. (*An den christlichen Adel*) [*LW* 44:137].
14. H. Bornkamm, *Luthers geistige Welt*, 4th ed. (Gütersloh, 1960), p. 239.
15. Holl, "Luther und das landesherrliche Kirchenregiment," p. 357, n. 1.

was now essentially a gift, not a goal. When Luther extravagantly lauded the acts of individual burghers and of the government, and when he gave them extremely broad powers, it was only because he thought in terms of *faithful* Christians and of a *Christian* magistracy.

There was, in other words, a split between the notions of the town in the late Middle Ages and those of Luther. This is clear, for example, in his letter of 1523 to the Christians of the imperial city of Worms,[16] in which he addressed them as a little band of true believers among the many indifferent and unbelieving. As a result, Luther's attitude was bound to explode the bonds of the old urban community.[17]

To be sure, the split is deeper from our viewpoint than it was for contemporaries. Luther himself, during the optimism of the first years when he was certain that the word would make its own path, did not sharply define the difference between the two conceptions, especially in his most wide-ranging works (as in the *Address to the Christian Nobility,* which actually seems to have been his missionary appeal to the cities). On the contrary, it seemed possible to him that the word would gradually conquer everywhere, if it could only get a footing among a few. He was still living in the medieval world of thought to such an extent that he could set this victory as his goal.[18] For his readers, with their Catholic background, it was completely natural in a certain sense to identify the Christian with the burgher. Thus in the eyes of townspeople the parallelism between Luther's antipathy for the Roman church and their own must have seemed clearer and more important than the difference in the foundations on which they built their arguments. Luther had built bridges to his urban readers, leading to an easier understanding of his teaching.

16. *WA,* Br 3, no. 651.
17. An important fact not recognized by A. Schultze, *Stadtgemeinde und Reformation.*
18. Luther's treatise *De instituendis ministris Ecclesiae* of 1523 is typical of his thought on this subject: *WA* 12:169 ff. [*LW* 40:7 ff.]. On this matter see also K. Müller, *Kirche, Gemeinde und Obrigkeit nach Luther* (Tübingen, 1910), pp. 57 ff.

2.

It is nonetheless a most significant fact that the two greatest theologians after Luther in the first generation of the Reformation, Zwingli and Bucer, were both citizens of free cities; and both differed with Luther at precisely those points of contact between urban thought and the Reformation where the gulf between Luther and the cities was most clear, i.e., in the concept of the church and in the basis of ethics.[19]

Fundamentally, of course, both stood on the same principles as Luther: salvation was exclusively a work of God, and for man there was no other way of coming to God than giving oneself in faith to him and being ready to follow his will unconditionally as revealed in Holy Scripture. But both of them insisted more strongly on that second condition, according to which the commandment was given to Christians to do the will of God and establish his kingdom. This disagreed with the conclusion drawn by Luther that, since the new life of the Christian never ceased to be a gift, its external form could never have more than provisional value. At this point Zwingli and Bucer set off on separate paths with regard to particular details. We shall try to assess for each of them the central idea that characterizes their mode of thought.

One of the principal themes in the theology of Zwingli, or at least the one that preoccupied him most profoundly in his last years, was the problem of how to form the relationship between the congregation of Christians and the civil community.[20] In this

19. We shall disregard the third great burgher among the theological leaders of the Reformation, Oecolampadius, of Basel. On him see E. Staehelin, *Das theologische Lebenswerk Johannes Oekolampads* (Leipzig, 1939).

20. For the following I have benefitted most profoundly from the chapter on Zwingli in the book by H. Kressner, *Schweizer Ursprünge des anglikanischen Staatskirchentums* (Gütersloh, 1953), pp. 14 ff. Of course, many faults are evident. The article by Erik Wolf, "Die Sozialtheologie Zwinglis," in *Festschrift G. Kisch* (Stuttgart, 1955), pp. 167–88, is especially stimulating. See in addition J. Kreutzer, *Zwinglis Lehre von der Obrigkeit* (Stuttgart, 1909); P. Meyer, "Zwinglis Soziallehren" (Diss., Zurich, 1921); A. Farner, *Die Lehre von Kirche und Staat bei Zwingli* (Tübingen, 1930); B. Brockelmann, "Das Corpus Christianum bei Zwingli" (Diss., Breslau, 1938); S. Rother, *Die religiösen und geistigen Grundlagen der Politik Huldrych Zwinglis* (Erlangen, 1956). It is typical that for this kind of problem none of the works cited is by a theologian.

75

regard he never considered the idea of a community of true believers, i.e., an invisible, true church.[21] This idea had once led Luther to propose an *ecclesiola in ecclesia*, but Zwingli, as far as we know, never dreamed of this possibility. On the contrary, this man from Zurich had in mind the church in its visible form, to which sinners also belonged, and whose membership encompassed the whole city. From the beginning of his activity as a reformer,[22] he had felt the need of maintaining the unity of the Christian community and the civil community, which Luther had brought together in a new way by teaching a novel doctrine of the church. At the end of his life Zwingli succeeded in describing this unity in a magisterial essay.[23]

Like the other great city-dwelling reformers, Bucer and Calvin,[24] Zwingli always pictured human society in terms of a body, an image drawn from antiquity and from primitive Christianity. He conceived of both the civil community and the church as a living organism composed of many members which worked together in close relationship.[25] And the civil and ecclesiastical communities formed a body not only individually but together as *ecclesia et populus*.[26] The church and the civil authorities were in effect bound together in the common goal of expanding the kingdom of

21. On this subject see Farner, *Die Lehre von Kirche und Staat bei Zwingli*, pp. 3 ff.

22. After the disputations of 1523, Zwingli obviously never had serious reservations about letting the magistracy carry out the Reformation. The contrary opinion of Farner (*Die Lehre von Kirche und Staat bei Zwingli*, especially pp. 103 ff.) does not seem fully convincing to me.

23. Erik Wolf speaks of the "synthetic thought" of Zwingli, "Sozialtheologie," p. 176. In fact, as Wolf has conclusively proved for several areas of Zwingli's theology, the idea of unity was part of the very structure of his thought.

24. For Bucer, see below. For Calvin, see J. Bohatec, *Calvins Lehre von Staat und Kirche* (Breslau, 1937), p. 163 et passim.

25. *ZW-CR* 2:547, lines 33 ff. (*Quo pacto ingenui*). The magistracy was one member of this body (see below). As a matter of course, Zwingli thought of it as an organ of the people. On this subject see Wolf, "Sozialtheologie," p. 184; *ZW-CR* 14:417, lines 7 f. (Beginning of the Preface to his Commentary on Jeremiah).

26. *ZW-CR* 14:419, lines 19 ff. See also the second source cited below in part IV, note 25. Thus the magistracy was a member of this body, as Zwingli insisted against the Anabaptists. *ZW-CR* 3:872, lines 38 ff. (*De vera et falsa religione*).

God[27] and of making the honor of God a reality.[28] To be sure, everyone did this in his own way;[29] but church and state aided one another through a kind of inner agreement in fulfilling their own parts of the common task. On the one hand, the magistracy was crucial for the vigor of the church.[30] It took care of external order[31] and especially regulated the discipline of the church by supporting congregational admonitions with civil punishments.[32] On the other hand, and this seemed to concern Zwingli even more, the church had to help the state in fulfilling its task.[33] It was in effect the best teacher of the townspeople;[34] without true religion no state could really live.[35] Only a faithful Christian, for example, made a good judge, for only he could hold himself free of bias and render justice.[36] Only Christians could govern with fairness and intelligence,[37] and the domination of a non-Christian was

27. Kreutzer, *Zwinglis Lehre von der Obrigkeit*, pp. 33 ff.

28. See, for example, *ZW-CR* 1:467, lines 1 f.

29. *ZW-CR* 3:868, lines 15 ff. (*De vera et falsa religione*). The civil authority is in the service of "human justice," while the church is in the service of "divine justice." On these two concepts of Zwingli we may now consult the fine work of Heinrich Schmid, *Zwinglis Lehre von der göttlichen und menschlichen Gerechtigkeit* (Zurich, 1959). With reference to the quotation from Zwingli, W. Eisinger ("Gesetz und Evangelium bei Huldrych Zwingli" [Diss., Heidelberg, 1957], p. 179, n. 31) correctly emphasizes that one should not conclude that the state was absorbed by the church.

30. *ZW-CR* 4/2:59 (*Fidei expositio*).

31. On this point see Schmid, *Zwinglis Lehre*, pp. 109 f., 228 ff.

32. *ZW-CR* 2:335, lines 11 and 15 ff. Later Zwingli clarified and again emphasized the necessity of cooperation between church admonitions and civil discipline. The church was to discipline its members only when the magistracy failed to do so. Cf. on this matter, F. Wendel, *L'Eglise de Strasbourg. Sa constitution et son organization, 1532–1535* (Paris, 1942), p. 157. When the magistracy was delinquent, the congregation was to turn to self-help to preserve the purity of the body of Christ. *ZW-CR* 4:31, lines 12 ff. Cf. also R. Ley, "Kirchenzucht bei Zwingli" (Diss., Zurich, 1948).

33. For the following see Schmid, *Zwinglis Lehre*, pp. 230 ff.

34. See the second citation in note 37 below. In addition, *ZW-CR* 8, no. 355 (Letter to Lambert and the brethren in Strasbourg).

35. *ZW-CR* 14:13, lines 39 ff. (Preface to the Commentary on Isaiah).

36. *ZW-Sch* 6/1:233 (*In Ev. Matth.*); *ZW-CR* 13:379, lines 28 ff. (*Ann. in Exodum*).

37. *ZW-CR* 3:867, lines 11 ff. (*De vera et falsa religione*). *ZW-CR* 2:329, lines 22 ff.; 2:330, lines 6 ff. This notion is also found in St. Augustine.

foolishness or madness.[38] "In summary, he who rules with God alone has the solidest and best empire, while he who rules according to his own whims has the worst and most unstable one."[39] For in such a state, where *one* spirit united the magistracy and the citizens,[40] true happiness would arrive[41] and real peace would reign.[42]

The Christian state was to find detailed instructions for a life of the Spirit in Holy Scripture. Such a state was characterized not only by a general Christian orientation but by direct obedience to the orders of God. To receive these orders, however, it was necessary to have a judge to interpret Scripture. Thus the keystone of the whole edifice appears in the figure of the *prophet*, the man who possesses full powers to proclaim God's will to the community and who in the last analysis guarantees the prosperity of the state.[43] This was the figure of Zwingli himself.

This ideal picture of the ecclesiastical-civil community led by the Spirit, this "theocracy," could not survive the defeat and death of its founder, if in fact it ever really existed in Zurich at all. His death at Kappel as an *episcopus in armis* was both the logical conclusion of his system and soon afterward the target of criticism among his friends.[44] A clearer separation of the areas of church and city and with it a certain reevaluation of the proper role of the church itself seemed called for.

---

38. *ZW-CR* 3:873, lines 9 ff. (*De vera et falsa religione*). Here Zwingli directly contradicted Luther who thought it completely possible that heathens could be better rulers than Christians. For this point see G. Hillerdal, *Gehorsam gegen Gott und Menschen* (Göttingen, 1954), p. 64.

39. *ZW-CR* 2:346, lines 15 ff.

40. *ZW-CR* 14:419, lines 32 ff. Cf. also the second reference in note 37 above.

41. *ZW-CR* 3:868, lines 29 ff. (*De vera et falsa religione*).

42. *ZW-CR* 2:331, lines 23 f.; *ZW-CR* 8, no. 355 (Letter to Lambert and the brethren at Strasbourg).

43. *ZW-Sch* 6/1:550 (*In Ev. Lucae*).

44. For example, E. Staehelin, *Briefe und Akten zum Leben Oekolampads* (Leipzig, 1934), no. 954; T. Schiess, *Briefwechsel der Brüder Ambrosius und Thomas Blaurer* (Freiburg i.B., 1908), vol. 1, no. 229. For the development of the relations between the church and the civil authority in Zurich after Kappel, see F. Blanke, *Der junge Bullinger* (Zurich, 1942), pp. 155 ff. and the bibliography listed there.

The stage was set for Martin Bucer's great period in the 1530s.[45] More deeply impressed by Luther than Zwingli had been, the Strasbourg reformer still found himself extremely close to the man from Zurich in his basic conception of the relationship between the church and the civic community. In his doctrine, too, the church and the magistracy stood beside each other bound together in the same office of leading men to Christ.[46] For it was the essential duty of governments to provide for the welfare of their subjects. Their most important task[47] was to encourage and to support the pure service of God, which led to the highest happiness. This was why Bucer believed that the magistrates ought to protect the church, persecute heretics, hire preachers, and cooperate in church discipline. Conversely he emphasized the usefulness of religious education for the prosperity of the state. He too was convinced that Christians made the best citizens.[48] No one could fill a public office more skillfully than a true Christian,[49] since he would not act selfishly but for the common welfare.[50] Thus Bucer's ideal conception was also one of intensive cooperation between the two powers.[51]

---

45. For the following, see above all the dissertation of W. Bofinger, "Oberdeutschtum und württembergische Reformation" (Diss., Tübingen, 1957). In addition, the still fundamental work by A. Lang, *Der Evangelienkommentar des Martin Bucers und die Grundzüge seiner Theologie* (Leipzig, 1900); see also W. Pauck, *Das Reich Gottes auf Erden* (Berlin, 1928); R. Schultz, "Martin Butzers Anschauung von der christlichen Obrigkeit" (Diss., Freiburg i.B., 1932); J. Courvoisier, "La notion d'Eglise chez Bucer dans son developpement historique" (Diss., Geneva, 1933); R. Stupperich, "Die Kirche in M. Bucers theologische Entwicklung," *Archiv für Reformationsgeschichte* 35 (1938): 81–101; idem, "M. Bucers Anschauungen von der Kirche," *Zeitschrift für systematische Theologie* 17 (1940): 131–48; and finally, Wendel, *L'Eglise de Strasbourg.*
46. Pauck, *Reich Gottes auf Erden*, p. 57.
47. *Scripta Anglicana* (R. Stupperich, ed., *Bibliographia bucerana* [Leipzig, 1950], no. 115), pp. 297 ff. For the foundation of the religious duty of the magistracy, Bucer, like Melanchthon, appealed to natural law.
48. "The more Christian and more rich in faith a man is, the more zealously he will obey the civil laws." *Confessio Tetrapolitana*, Art. 23.
49. "This is why no one can better assume the functions of the magistracy than the most Christian and most pious people. It was doubtless for this reason that the ancient Christian emperors appointed bishops and other clergy to the magistracy." Ibid.
50. Pauck, *Reich Gottes auf Erden*, p. 42.
51. Wendel, *L'Eglise de Strasbourg*, pp. 165, 171 ff.

Yet Bucer saw more clearly than Zwingli that the magistracy could refuse this cooperation. For decades Bucer struggled with the Council of Strasbourg and learned a great deal from these bitter experiences.[52] In addition, Bucer always emphasized more strongly than Zwingli the limits of magisterial competence. The state should regulate the external actions of men but should not invade the hearts or faith of its subjects.[53] Influenced by Oecolampadius, Bucer's church ordinances combined state control of the church with the constitution of the community.[54] And Bucer was even willing to transfer the duty of church discipline totally to the community.[55] Finally, in view of the laxity of the Strasbourg Council, he tentatively[56] even put into effect Luther's old idea of separating the serious Christians from the others.

All of this was possible only because Bucer's conception of the church differed slightly from that of Zwingli. Bucer did speak frequently of the visible church. He believed, however, that it contained the true church, the community of the chosen, and that the true church left the mark of its rules for living on the visible church. The Holy Spirit dwelt within the church. Thus the invisibility and visibility of the church appeared curiously intertwined. His conception of its holiness was astonishingly direct. In such questions Calvin was the first to bring true clarity to the Reform tradition.[57]

52. For all of the details see W. Köhler, *Zürcher Ehegericht und Genfer Konsistorium* (Leipzig, 1932–1942), 2:349 ff.

53. Cf. Wendel, *L'Eglise de Strasbourg*, p. 251.

54. Cf. the summary in R. Schultz, "Butzers Anschauung von der christlichen Obrigkeit," pp. 10 ff.; as well as the article by E. W. Kohls, "Ein Abschnitt aus Martin Bucers Entwurf für die Ulmer Kirchenordnung vom Jahr 1531," *Blätter für württembergische Kirchengeschichte* 60/61 (1960/61): 193, n. 95.

55. On the disciplinary ordinance of Ziegenhain, see W. Maurer, *Gemeindezucht, Gemeindeamt, Konfirmation* (Kassel, 1940), pp. 17 ff.

56. For this subject, cf. W. Bellardi, *Die Geschichte der "Christlichen Gemeinschaft" in Strassburg (1546–1550)* (Leipzig, 1934).

57. For these criticisms, cf. also the contentions of Bofinger, "Oberdeutschtum," pp. 13 ff. It seems to me, however, that Bofinger relies too uncritically on Luther as a criterion to gauge the faults of Bucer's system. He did not consider the possibility that Bucer, in taking this position, might have had a real, personal, and theologically justifiable idea. In this way Bofinger destroys his chances of drawing correct conclusions from his seminal discovery, which in other respects is generally so instructive. His work has decisively influenced this study of mine.

Bucer described the church as a perfect model of community, as "the most perfect, most friendly, and most faithful brotherhood, community, and union."[58] Each member had been assigned his place by the Lord, and all were now to compete in helping each other and thereby benefit the whole body.[59] This community's single most characteristic quality was unity,[60] and the communal life was directed by one principle: love. Love was the *vitae magistra* [teacher of life].[61] All laws, both biblical and profane, and all the institutions of man unite, if they are good, in this one principle.[62] Conversely, the church should banish all such ceremonies and ordinances that did not spring from love. When Bucer rejected Catholic institutions,[63] it was not because they were a dangerous seduction into works-righteousness, but primarily because they

---

58. *Von der wahren Seelsorge* (Stupperich, *Bibliographia bucerana*, no. 59b), p. 6. For the following, cf. especially Pauck, *Reich Gottes auf Erden*, pp. 13 ff.

59. *Scripta Anglicana* (Stupperich, *Bibliographia bucerana*, no. 115), p. 267; *Von der wahren Seelsorge* (Stupperich, *Bibliographia bucerana*, no. 59b), p. 7; *De Regno Christi*, p. 13. "Thus one can further conclude that nothing should be considered a Christian act if it does not somehow serve the interests of one's neighbor; and that every work is appropriate to Christian action to the extent that it brings advantage to one's neighbor." *Confessio Tetrapolitana*, Art. 6. Thus the deacons were even responsible for guiding the poor into the service of the community. *De Regno Christi*, pp. 151 f.

60. In the conflict over the Lord's Supper, the real motive of Bucer's actions was the unity of the church. On the occasions when he described this unity, one might even mistake him for a Catholic. Cf., for example, Schiess, *Ambrosius und Thomas Blaurer*, vol. 2, no. 940. Of course, a decisive difference remained in that this unity was realized in attitude and not in organization. W. Pauck, "Calvin and Butzer," *Journal of Religion* 9 (1929): 255: "Butzer was a Catholic with a Protestant heart."

61. *Epheser Kommentar* (Stupperich, *Bibliographia bucerana*, no. 17), fol. 38a.

62. *Ev. Komm.* (Stupperich, *Bibliographia bucerana*, no. 14), p. 341; ibid., p. 115. All laws are only worthy of the name if they are "derived from and follow the most important law," that is, the law of love. *De Regno Christi*, p. 266.

63. *Ev. Komm.* (Stupperich, *Bibliographia bucerana*, no. 28a), p. 116. One can easily see how different Bucer's fundamental conception was from that of Luther by comparing the articles of the *Confessio Tetrapolitana* on monastic oaths or on fasting, for example, with the corresponding articles of the *Confessio Augustana*. While the Lutheran confession found these Catholic practices faulty primarily because they led to works-righteousness, Bucer's main objection was that monastic oaths separated man from society and released him from his most noble duty, to love his neighbor; in a similar vein, Bucer objected that fasting was, at best, only an indirect service to one's neighbor.

had no value for the community. For that reason the services of love seemed to him indispensable for the church. Giving alms to the poor[64] and, above all, warning and punishing sinners, i.e., the office of deacon or the man in charge of discipline, were just as valuable as the office of preaching.[65] Love was, therefore, the fundamental law of the Christian life, the completion of the road of faith.[66] Bucer's ethic was essentially a community ethic.[67]

It is clear that Bucer wanted to apply his ideas to the domain of the state. This became obvious in 1549 when, freed from the obligations that had kept him in Strasbourg, he went to England and, with a commission to draw up a new order, gave free expression to his ideas. In *De Regno Christi* he drew a grand picture of a community, vigorous because of the intimate intertwining and unity of ecclesiastical and civil life, a community grounded in the most profound forces of the Christian faith, obedient to God's word, and ruled as a result by public spirit.[68]

3.

It would be foolish if we tried to derive the differences which we have discovered between Luther and the fathers of the so-called Reformed theology simply from the fact that Luther was the subject of a prince while Bucer and Zwingli were burghers.[69] Who

64. *De Regno Christi*, p. 143.

65. Bofinger, "Oberdeutschtum," pp. 33 ff. It is well known that Bucer, like Oecolampadius, wanted to revive the offices of primitive Christianity, and he based the necessity of these offices on the New Testament. Cf. on this point W. Maurer, *Gemeindezucht, Gemeindeamt, Konfirmation*, pp. 36 ff. Yet Zwingli, who had been the first to conceive of imitating the primitive Christian offices (in a letter written in 1528 to Blarer [*ZW-CR* 9, no. 720, p. 455, lines 30 ff.]), was also more aware of the real distance between the two ages than were the reformers of Basel or Strasbourg. In possessing this kind of historical sense, Zwingli was not far removed from Luther. On Luther cf. *WA*, TR 4, no. 4342.

66. *Eph. Komm.* (Stupperich, *Bibliographia bucerana*, no. 17), fol. 21a.

67. In energetically concentrating on this one thought, which he knew to be solidly based on the Bible, Bucer was unique in the sixteenth century. To be sure, the general tendency, the interest in the community, was common to both Bucer and Zwingli. See, for example, the citation in note 41 above.

68. *De Regno Christi*, p. 292.

69. On the question of the difference between lordship and community, see note 35 in part I. H. J. Grimm, in "Die Beziehungen Luthers und Melanchthons zu den Bürgern," in *Luther und Melanchthon*, ed. W. H. Neuser

would assert that human decisions, and especially decisions regarding theology, law, or church politics, can be explained simply with sociological data? Instead, these decisions were motivated by both personal and impersonal factors, like temperament, the sense of responsibility and spontaneity, as well as external influences and constraints of various sorts, in such a way as to form an inexplicable nexus. We can list, particularly in this case, a whole series of factors that helped to determine the special character of the theology of the reformers from Upper Germany and Switzerland.

It is essential to recognize at once that Zwingli and Bucer were both *humanists*.[70] The political ideas of Zwingli in particular were certainly influenced by humanist thought.

The northern humanists had preserved the republican ideal of the early Italian Renaissance.[71] They were thoroughly conditioned by the idea of *publica utilitas*[72] as well as by the conception of the state as an organism. Hence Erasmus, for example, invested the state with religious splendor and incorporated the church within it as an educational institution. Absolutist ideas were al-

---

(Munich, 1961), goes so far as to call these two Wittenberg reformers "burghers." It is clear, however, that such a term lacks precision. Grimm has also neglected the fact that if the term is made more precise, the Reformation is really the end of a period in the history of the German townspeople, rather than the sign of something new. This has been shown by H. Heimpel in his essay "Das Wesen des deutschen Spätmittelalters," in *Der Mensch in seiner Gegenwart* (Göttingen, 1954).

70. For our purposes we may disregard the contention of Köhler that the differences between Zwingli and Luther stemmed from the fact that the former was trained as a realist while the latter was trained as a nominalist, a thesis which as far as I can see has found very little support. We also receive no help from Lang's theory that the peculiarity of Bucer's theology is based on his relations with German mysticism, although it is high time that this theory be tested!

71. For the whole problem see W. Maurer, *Das Verhältnis des Staates zur Kirche nach humanistischer Anschauung* (Giessen, 1930); F. Geldner, *Die Staatsauffassung und Fürstenlehre des Erasmus von Rotterdam* (Berlin, 1930); H. Treinen, "Studien zur Idee der Gemeinschaft bei Erasmus von Rotterdam" (Diss., Saarbrücken, 1955).

72. Of course, this idea was not simply of humanist origins. For the contrary view, see Maurer, *Das Verhältnis*, p. 15, n. 1. And now see the observations of Maurer on just this point in his review of the edition of Bucer's works by Wendel (in *Archiv für Reformationsgeschichte* 51 [1960]: 117 ff.).

ready beginning to dawn. Erasmus, and doubtless Wimpfeling too, found their ideal constitution in a monarchy[73] whose rulers were supposed to be responsible for the welfare and freedom of their subjects and therefore morally limited. This way seemed to guarantee most effectively that *tranquillitas,* or inner peace of the commonwealth, on which the humanists placed the highest value.

The organic conception of civic life, the readiness to unite the tasks of the church with those of the state in a direct and positive bond, and finally the extremely utilitarian attitude shown in these matters—all of these humanist ideas appear again in Zwingli and Bucer.[74] It remains an open question, of course, to what extent the reformers were dependent on humanism and to what extent they only found their own ideas confirmed and clarified by it.[75]

In any event, they rejected the political doctrine of Erasmus at important points. Let us take note of a remarkable fact: Zwingli and Bucer[76] regarded the republican ideal as a dogma higher than all other considerations.[77] Both of them expressed themselves often regarding the value of the various forms of government, and Zwingli once even compared them explicitly among themselves.[78] They never left any doubt that for them a monarchy in which the

73. See the quotation of Erasmus in the work by Maurer, *Das Verhält-nis,* p. 18.

74. The humanist ideal of peace also had a certain importance for these reformers, noticeably as early as 1516 in Zwingli's *Labyrinth.* For Bucer's contact with the political doctrines of Erasmus, cf. *DS* 1:38, n. 16.

75. In a slightly different context Kressner put it strikingly: "It was not because of his humanism that Zwingli put morals and rules of conduct in the center of his intellectual world; to the contrary, it was his moralism that led him to seek the company of kindred spirits, like Seneca, Cicero, and Erasmus." *Schweizer Ursprünge,* p. 19. Yet this insight should not be pushed so far as to deny the educational function of humanism altogether. There are some interesting although brief and casual remarks on the subject of "Humanism and the City" in H. Schmidt, *Die deutschen Städte-chroniken als Spiegel des bürgerlichen Selbstverständnisses im Spätmittel-alter* (Göttingen, 1958), p. 13.

76. Like many other burghers among the humanists.

77. M. Schmidt also draws this distinction between Zwingli and Erasmus in his review of Kressner in the *Archiv für Reformationsgeschichte* 48 (1957): 135 f.

78. In the preface to his commentary on Isaiah written in 1529. See also the section "Magistratus" in the *Fidei expositio, ZW-Sch* 4/2:59 f. Here, of course, one can feel Zwingli's deference to the intended recipient of the letter, Francis I of France.

ruler took no account of his subjects was thoroughly reprehensible.[79] For both of them the constitution of their own city, the system which Zwingli called *aristocratia*, provided the criterion for judgment.[80] It was their ideal since all sides were represented in government. This balance seemed to guarantee that the best actually did govern.[81] No one, therefore, could follow his own selfish interest uncontrolled.[82] The people themselves took part in the direction of affairs, and in that way the responsibility of all for the common welfare was strengthened.[83]

Zwingli's and Bucer's views of the state[84] were obviously determined in large measure by their citizenship in free cities and by their profound attachment to the urban structure. In addition, it is

79. Zwingli expressly disagreed with the preference for monarchy shown by ancient writers. *ZW-CR* 14:10, lines 34 ff. In the preface to his commentary on Isaiah he drew up a whole series of arguments against monarchy. Elsewhere he called on his listeners zealously to guard their independence. *ZW-CR* 13:406, lines 25 ff. (*Ann. in Exodum*). Zwingli was especially concerned to demonstrate that princely power received its legitimation from its subjects. *ZW-CR* 3:446, line 7 (*Wer Ursach gebe*). Zwingli's writings show no lack of hostile remarks about the princes of his time. *ZW-Sch* 6/1:563 (*In Ev. Lucae*). On this point cf. W. Köhler, "Zwingli und das Reich," *Welt als Geschichte* 6 (1940): 1–14. Bucer was probably more favorably inclined to monarchy, but Pauck goes badly astray in labeling him a monarchist. On this point cf. H. Baron, "Calvinist Republicanism and its Historical Roots," *Church History* 8 (1939): 38, n. 18. Bucer himself stated his view clearly enough. *Enarr. in Libr. Iudicum*, in the edition of the Psalms commentary of 1554 (Stupperich, *Bibliographia bucerana*, no. 25d), fol. Iiia. In *De Regno Christi* he provided all kinds of horrible examples of the tyranny of absolute monarchs (pp. 125 ff.) and proposed calling the Parliament in England again. Schultz, "Butzers Anschauung von der christlichen Obrigkeit," p. 87. He also explained his position in detail in the "Advice to Hamburg" of 1545. H. von Schubert, "Die Beteilung der dänisch-holsteinischen Landesfürsten am hamburgischen Kapitelstreit und das Gutachten Martin Bucers von 1545," *Schriften des Vereins für schleswig-holsteinische Kirchengeschichte* 2/3 (1904/05): 51 f.
80. Zwingli stated this directly. *ZW-CR* 14:9, lines 17 ff. For Bucer cf. above all the "Advice to Hamburg" cited in the preceding note.
81. *ZW-CR* 14:11, lines 11 ff.; 14:9, lines 26 f.
82. Ibid., p. 11, lines 4 ff. During his early years Bucer even called monarchy a direct result of God's wrath. *Ev. Komm.* 1530 (Stupperich, *Bibliographia bucerana*, no. 28), fol. 57b.
83. *ZW-CR* 14:11, lines 13 ff. (Preface to Isaiah). For Bucer, his request for naturalization in Strasbourg in 1523 provides a characteristic example of his thought. *DS* 1:302, lines 5 ff.
84. And also those of Calvin. Cf. his comments on the constitutional question, quoted in Bohatec, *Calvins Lehre von Staat und Kirche*, pp. 124 ff. In addition, see the article by Baron, "Calvinist Republicanism and its Historical Roots."

possible that humanism and many other forces affected them: Zwingli, who, of course, was not a burgher by birth, was influenced perhaps by the Swiss environment in general;[85] Bucer, through his membership in the Dominican Order, may have been influenced by the political doctrines of Thomas Aquinas, which he knew.

From their ties with civic life and thought we can understand why both Zwingli and Bucer were deeply involved in politics.[86] For them life as a theologian and churchman was inseparably bound up with life as a citizen. It is not just a symptom of their temperament that they plunged actively into the internal and external affairs of their cities[87] and from that arena became involved in high politics. How carefully Zwingli the strategist planned and furthered the spread of the Reformation in Switzerland and southern Germany! How skillfully Bucer politically maneuvered the compromise in the fight over the Lord's Supper! It was characteristic and appropriate that Philip of Hesse carried on his famous and highly political correspondence with precisely these two theologians from free cities and not with Luther, who could even say, "It would be more godly to increase agriculture and

85. In this context scholars often refer to Zwingli's national feelings. Kreutzer speaks with particular solemnity of the "pride that rises and trembles in the heart of the Swiss at the mention of freedom." *Zwinglis Lehre von der Obrigkeit,* p. 46. It seems to me, however, that the republicanism of the *burgher* Zwingli has been overly neglected, and, as our line of argument has shown, this is not the same as national feeling. The parallels with Bucer are suggestive. I would especially reject the contention of the otherwise instructive article by H. Dreyfuss, "Die Entwicklung eines politischen Gemeinsinns in der schweizerischen Eidgenossenschaft und der Politiker Ulrich Zwingli," *Revue d'Histoire Suisse* 6 (1926): 61–127, 145–93, in which the author, in my opinion, makes too sharp a distinction between the situation in Switzerland and that prevailing in the Upper German cities; e.g., pp. 77, 145, 182.

86. Bucer had a well-informed and lively interest in matters of political economy. Cf. on this point G. Klingenberg, "Das Verhältnis Calvins zu Bucer untersucht auf Grund der wirtschaftsethischen Bedeutung beider Reformatoren" (Diss., Bonn, 1912). In *De Regno Christi* there is a whole chapter entitled "De reformanda mercatura," pp. 247 ff.

87. Kressner's description of these relationships is not completely satisfying. For example, he says, "The communal character of the German city . . . made it possible for Zwingli to bridge the gap between the spiritual and secular spheres and to control the propagation of the Reformation, the project that meant most to him." *Schweizer Ursprünge,* p. 33, n. 1. This seems to neglect the fact that every sixteenth-century burgher, at least in Switzerland and Upper Germany, "automatically" became politically oriented.

decrease commerce."[88] Luther could not see himself as sharing responsibility for the actions of his government;[89] on the contrary, for him all authority, even that of towns, was "established." The idea that magistracy and subjects were theoretically one was not basic to Luther's concept of the state.[90]

Zwingli and Bucer were obviously bound to the urban world. With that much said, we may be permitted to suspect that the influence of this world view is found at those points which distinguished their theology from Luther's. Those points are, as we have seen, the generally high value that they placed on the external organization of the church, the interest in the intimate connection between church and state, and finally the communal idea. It seems possible to prove the accuracy of this suspicion at least indirectly.

Probably as with the beginnings of all great historical movements stemming from one source, a more profound understanding of the first years of the Reformation shows a period of gathering followed by a period of dispersion. All of the important Protestant theologians of the first generation found their own individuality and independence only after going through a period of more or less close dependence on Luther. This is true for Melanchthon and Carlstadt, and possibly even for Müntzer, but in any event certainly for Zwingli and Bucer.[91] With Zwingli and Bucer the development away from Luther is easy to observe in terms of the questions we have been dealing with. They initially emphasized the true church as the communion of saints, and both were concerned to

88. *WA* 6:466, lines 40 f. (*An den christlichen Adel*) [*LW* 44:214].

89. In K. Aland's useful article, "Martin Luther als Staatsbürger," in *Kirchengeschichtliche Entwürfe* (Gütersloh, 1960), pp. 420–51, it is striking how few documents show Luther engaged in genuinely political actions.

90. A passage like *WA* 19:640, lines 22 ff. [*LW* 46:113], shows how far Luther was from such thoughts. He treats the constitutional limitation of the kings of France and Denmark as if it were a distant matter of no concern to him. Or, to take an even better example, *WA*, TR 4, no. 4342, in which Luther calls the constitution of the empire an aristocracy (compare this to Zwingli!).

91. In the following sentences I follow the suggestions of the work by Bofinger, "Oberdeutschtum," although with a different emphasis. Of course, he was concerned only with Bucer.

preserve the independence of the church from the government. Yet both changed, Zwingli following a fairly direct path, Bucer with many intermediate steps, so that at the end of their lives they were drafting great essays on church and state.[92]

Confrontation with the Anabaptists and fanatics only furthered this development for the two reformers of Zurich and Strasbourg. Still it was primarily their lively interest in the communal church, even before the appearance of the sects, that prevented Zwingli and Bucer from joining the cause of the Anabaptists. These splinter groups shattered the unity of the town.[93] This concern for the communal church grew with Zwingli and Bucer as the magistrates of Zurich and Strasbourg began to establish the Reformation. On this occasion the councils themselves appealed to the ministers to cooperate or even to take part in some of the decisions. This was the moment when the ancient ideas of the urban community were reviving in the towns, ideas which now called on the Reformation for confirmation and for a new kind of foundation. The characteristic theology of the Swiss and Upper German reformers seemed at essential points to be a response to this call.[94] The actual urban communities which Zwingli and Bucer confronted

92. The massively documented contention of Farner, *Die Lehre von Kirche und Staat bei Zwingli*, that Zwingli's opinions underwent a development has been rejected by Brockelmann, "Das Corpus Christianum," and Kressner, *Schweizer Ursprünge*. Yet neither of them has really based his opposition on the sources. It seems to me, therefore, that Farner's demonstration, or at least its fundamental structure, remains valid, especially since Zwingli himself noticed this development. Cf. his comments on the words of Luther: "Regnum Christi non est externum"; and the position he took on this subject in a letter to Blarer in 1528. *ZW-CR* 9, no. 720, pp. 451 f. Erik Wolf, "Sozialtheologie," also decides against Kressner, p. 181, n. 52. On Bucer, cf. Wendel, *L'Eglise de Strasbourg*, p. 163; and for the whole subject, Lang, *Die Evangelienkommentar des Martin Bucers*.

93. On this point, finally, see the convincing remarks of J. Yoder, *Täufertum und Reformation in der Schweiz* (Karlsruhe, 1962), passim. For the reformers at Strasbourg, cf., for example, the memorandum of the preachers to the council on 23 January 1529, opposing the Anabaptists; in Krebs and Rott, *Quellen zur Geschichte der Täufer der Stadt Strassburg* (Gütersloh, 1959), 1:202 f.

94. It is clear that the "classical" or characteristic dogma of Zwinglianism, namely, Zwingli's understanding of the Supper and of the sacraments, is not oriented solely toward urban thought. One can, of course, ask whether Lutheran and Reformed systems are really so profoundly different on this point (Bofinger, "Oberdeutschtum," also opposes this traditional distinction, p. 75). The controversy over the Supper seems more a "tragic accident"

had strongly favored the shifts in their theology which we have described. *To understand and appreciate the characteristics of this theology, therefore, one must see it as the result of the Reformation message filtered through the mentality of the free city.*

This thesis[95] becomes even more convincing when we turn to the content of the theology itself. As we are coming to see, the essence of the theological evolution of Zwingli and Bucer was the increasingly clear conception of church and civic community as one body. It was at just this point that Luther's doctrine seemed most deeply foreign to the mentality of the city. In logically linking the concept of the church to justification by grace alone and by faith alone, he had exploded the unity of the medieval town.

At this point Zwingli and Bucer corrected Luther. Compared with Luther, their thought was much more concerned with the totality than with the individual. By insisting more strongly on ideas of community and organism, they truly succeeded in deepening the position of Luther with regard to the concepts of church and state. The mode of thought of the town permitted them to

---

that set off the conflict of Luther and Zwingli (as W. Köhler contended, *Zwingli und Luther* [Leipzig, 1924], 1:551, n. 2) or, more precisely, an accident that brought to light the formal difference between the Lutheran and Reformed Reformations. Nonetheless, after the ancient sacramental doctrine had been destroyed—primarily under humanist instigation—and after the possibility of obtaining salvation through external rituals had come under fire, Zwingli and Bucer restored the communal idea to a dominant role in their own versions of baptism and the Supper. In baptism the infant was admitted into the Christian community, and the Supper was a communal meal (on the "churchly dimension" of Zwingli's doctrine of the Supper, see the helpful exposition of J. Courvoisier, *Zwingli, théologien réformé* [Neuchatel, 1965], pp. 48–84, especially p. 83). Because of Luther's emphasis on consoling and strengthening the isolated and troubled Christian, could it be that his doctrine of the Lord's Supper was considered overly individualistic by Upper German and Swiss theologians and that this might account for the antipathy that these theologians, and especially their congregations, felt for this Lutheran doctrine? This would be an area worthy of more reflection and research. For Bucer's communal ideas about the Supper, the appropriate chapter in *Grund und Ursach* (1524) is particularly characteristic. *DS* 1:241 ff. For the uniqueness of Luther's doctrine, finally, see A. Peters, *Realpräsenz. Luthers Zeugnis von Christi Gegenwart im Abendmahl* (Berlin, 1960), pp. 156 ff.

95. The thesis is not exactly new. Even Leopold von Ranke, *Deutsche Geschichte im Zeitalter der Reformation* (Munich, 1925–26), book 5, chapter 3, made reference (the earliest known to me) to the "republican" sentiments which formed the background for the Reformation in Switzerland. This idea has appeared occasionally since then, but no one has ever examined it to see if it is valid.

recognize in certain regards how the church had been organized during the age of primitive Christianity—a point that had escaped Luther—and they appealed justifiably to that age. On the other hand, one can better understand the obscurities and difficulties which the reformers encountered in their explanation of the church and in their doctrine of justification if one bears in mind that they were fighting to adapt their Reformation message to the urban mentality and that they continued to take account of the social order of the town.

Thus Zwingli and Bucer from a certain point of view remained more trapped than Luther in medieval modes of thought.[96] Yet one can certainly not say that they betrayed the Reformation in favor of the city. In effect, the Reformation whenever it prevailed destroyed certain essential conditions of the medieval town, the miniature *corpus christianum*. Both reformers taught that the holiness of the city did not have its most profound basis in being a holy community, guaranteeing salvation to those who were a part of it; but instead by being the place where God's word was proclaimed and believed and faithfully obeyed. In Zwingli's figure of the "prophet" and in Bucer's doctrine of governing the *regnum Christi* by the word of God, the medieval sacred society essentially dissolved.

IV. LUTHERANISM AND ZWINGLIANISM

1.

We have thus far treated the Reformation of the imperial cities as if it constituted a unity. This picture is, however, imprecise, and we must provide certain nuances. In the 1520s and 1530s the free

---

96. For the problem of the extent to which Zwingli's ideas were still medieval, cf. the work by Brockelmann, "Das Corpus Christianum," and the remarks of Heinrich Schmid, *Zwinglis Lehre*, pp. 260 ff. Certainly Zwingli was "more urban" and hence "more medieval" than Bucer. The "old-fashioned" reluctance of Zwingli to destroy the unity of the urban community is hardly found in Luther at all, and Bucer was able to overcome his scruples in this regard. Conversely, Luther's willingness to set the state free is missing in Zwingli. Luther, because of both his origins and his profession, found it easier to neglect social realities in his theological thought than the two pastors from free cities. The city of Wittenberg, for which he was indeed concerned, "was lacking in the traditions of social structure and spirituality of the late medieval German city." H. Schöffler, *Die Reformation* (Bochum, 1936), p. 24. However, even for Luther, the ancient *corpus christianum* did not disappear entirely.

Protestant cities split into two groups, a large group following Zwingli and Bucer, and a smaller one, Luther.[1]

The imperial cities of the North, Lübeck and Goslar, were Lutheran, as were the other large cities of the German North which enjoyed a *de facto* freedom in the sixteenth century: Bremen, Hamburg, Lüneburg, Braunschweig, Göttingen, and so on. In addition, the Protestant imperial cities of Franconia were also Lutheran. Nuremberg was the most prominent of these, followed by her satellites, Windsheim and Weissenburg. The Franconian cities within the Swabian imperial circle were also Lutheran: Dinkelsbühl, Schwäbisch Hall, and Heilbronn. In the early 1540s, Regensburg, Schweinfurt, Rothenburg, and Donauwörth joined the Lutheran ranks. The cities of Hesse and the Palatinate in the West, especially Frankfurt and Worms, and in the East, Nördlingen, maintained a denominationally intermediate position.

On the other hand, among the Protestant imperial cities in the German Southwest, the so-called Upper German Cities of the Swabian or Alemannic region, from Esslingen in the north to Constance in the south, from Augsburg in the east to Strasbourg in the west, as well as the free Swiss cities, all followed Zwingli and Bucer.[2] The imperial city of Reutlingen was the single exception.[3]

1. It is an obvious fault of the book by A. Schultze, *Stadtgemeinde und Reformation* (Tübingen, 1918), that it misses this fact and that it expressly and intentionally excludes the Swiss Reformation from consideration (p. 7).
2. Although we know little of its Protestant past, even an imperial city as small as the Baden city of Gengenbach shows "Reformed" influence. Their beautiful catechism, which has survived to this day, shows that the Gengenbach reformers were followers of Bucer. J. Sauer, "Der evangelische Katechismus von Gengenbach," *Freiburger Diözesan-Archiv,* n.s. 21 (1920): 193–207, claims otherwise, but he is not sufficiently familiar with the theology of Strasbourg. See on this subject E. W. Kohls, *Der evangelische Katechismus von Gengenbach aus dem Jahre 1545* (Heidelberg, 1963).
3. In the conflict over the Supper, Matthäus Alber, Reutlingen's reformer, remained loyal to Luther, and the city signed the Confession of Augsburg in 1530. On this point see M. Brecht, "Matthäus Albers Theologie," *Blätter für württembergische Kirchengeschichte* 62 (1962): 63–97. Nevertheless, the burghers of Reutlingen deliberately maintained contact with Zwingli (*ZW-CR* 10, no. 913) and with Bucer (J. Hartmann, *Matthäus Alber der Reformator der Reichsstadt Reutlingen* [Tübingen, 1863], pp. 117 ff.). And at Reutlingen they too organized a *repurgatio templi* (letter of Alber to Zwingli, 21 February 1531: *ZW-CR* 11, no. 1170) and it was precisely its populace that held to as simple a divine service as possible. Hartmann, *Matthäus Alber,* p. 104.

What are the identifying marks of a "Reformed" city?[4] Among their external features they have in common the austerity of their divine service,[5] the opposition to images, but above all the opposition of their pastors to the Lutheran doctrine of communion. In addition, the citizens of these cities worked with particular energy to perfect and consolidate the spiritual and moral life of the ecclesiastical and urban communities, to renovate public charity, public instruction, and civil discipline. Anticipating Calvin, they often set as their ideal a *civitas christiana*, or holy city, and in several places they came quite close to realizing this goal.[6] But for our purpose it is most important to note the extremely significant role which the *lay element* played in all these activities. Of course, the late medieval tradition of strict civil control of morals in these cities probably accounts for the active participation of council members in the direction of church affairs[7] and for the great importance of lay offices[8] in the church.[9] But, in addition, the Reformation in

4. In what follows we utilize this essentially imprecise and anachronistic term (as is well known, the Book of Concord of 1580 calls the "Lutheran" churches *reformatae nostrae ecclesiae*) for lack of a better one to describe the peculiarities of the Upper German and Swiss Reformation. In doing so we are not forgetting the differences between Zwingli and Bucer, which we have mentioned· above, nor are we forgetting that it was more Bucer's doctrine than Zwingli's which prevailed in Upper Germany.

5. H. Waldenmaier, *Die Entstehung der evangelischen Gottesdienstordnungen Süddeutschlands im Zeitalter der Reformation* (Halle, 1916), pp. 26 ff.

6. B. Moeller, "Die Kirche in den evangelischen freien Städten Oberdeutschlands im Zeitalter der Reformation," *Zeitschrift für die Geschichte des Oberrheins* 112 (1964): 67–82.

7. Of course, control of the church by the council was perhaps even more strict elsewhere, for example, in the entirely Lutheran city of Nuremberg or in Lübeck after 1535. For the cities of Upper Germany see the second volume of the work by W. Köhler, *Zürcher Ehegericht und Genfer Konsistorium* (Leipzig, 1932–1942), which deals individually with most of these cities. This book of Köhler's is the first to treat comprehensively the Reformation of these imperial cities of Southwest Germany as a special type within the Reformation movement. Since then I have attempted in my study "Die Kirche in den evangelischen freien Städten Oberdeutschlands im Zeitalter der Reformation" (see note 6 above) to develop and explore further Köhler's results.

8. Of course, the institution of "supervisor of morals" appeared in the Reformation of other imperial cities. It played a role in Bugenhagen's ecclesiastical ordinances (Hamburg, 1529; Lübeck, 1531) and appeared as early as 1526 in Schwäbisch Hall with Brenz. Taking issue with the article by E. Wolf, "Johannes Bugenhagen, Gemeinde und Amt," in *Peregrinatio* (Munich, 1954), pp. 257–78, Lau is right when he states that here, as well as elsewhere in his activation of the community, Bugenhagen was able to build on late-medieval customs. F. Lau, "Der Bauernkrieg und das angebliche Ende der Lutherischen Reformation als spontaner Volksbewegung," *Luther-*

the cities of Upper Germany was especially characterized by the participation of the people, "the common man," who played an active role in ecclesiastical innovation as never before. Indeed, this participation was not limited to the introduction of the Reformation but involved its maintenance as well. Passions were aroused in an astonishing fashion, each city wishing to conserve its own peculiar character, not only in relation to Roman Catholicism but also in relation to Lutheranism. We can even state that the decades-long retention of the "Reformed" elements in these cities was due less to the efforts of the theologians than to the efforts of the laity, the magistrates, and especially the populace. For the Upper German cities at least, it is false to maintain that the people took no part in the theological disputes of the sixteenth century.[10]

In several of these cities both before and after 1530 violent debates occurred between Zwinglian and Lutheran preachers mainly over the subject of communion. Document after document shows that the people took lively interest in these conflicts and that they regularly sided with the Zwinglians. The crudest, almost comic, testimony comes from the most populous city of the Reformation, Augsburg.[11] If a Zwinglian or an Anabaptist preached, he had sixteen thousand listeners; a Lutheran, on the other hand, could attract only six or seven.[12] It was under these circumstances

---

Jahrbuch 26 (1959): 132. This question deserves more comprehensive and detailed study. Still, as Köhler shows (see note 7 above), lay offices were *regularly* established in the Upper German cities.

9. This is conjectured by Ritter in his instructive and penetrating review of Köhler's book mentioned in note 7 above. *Archiv für Reformationsgeschichte* 40 (1943): 72–89 (81).

10. As is erroneously maintained on several occasions in the two works by E. W. Zeeden, "Grundlagen und Wege der Konfessionsbildung in Deutschland im Zeitalter der Glaubenskämpfe," *Historische Zeitschrift* 185 (1958): 249–99, and *Katholische Überlieferungen in den Lutherischen Kirchenordnungen des 16. Jahrhunderts* (Münster, 1959).

11. G. Schmoller, *Das Städtewesen in älterer Zeit* (Bonn, 1922), p. 87; E. Keyser, *Bevölkerungsgeschichte Deutschlands*, 3rd ed. (Leipzig, 1943), pp. 313 ff., furnishes other statistical data concerning the population.

12. G. Kawerau, "Zur Reformationsgeschichte Augsburgs," *Beiträge zur bayerischen Kirchengeschichte* 2 (1896): 131 ff. Naturally the numbers are exaggerated to the point of absurdity! Still, the substance of the report is confirmed from all sides. Compare, for example, the report from the Imperial Diet of 1530, quoted by W. Maurer, "Zum geschichtlichen Verständnis der Abendmahlsartikel in der Confessio Augustana," in *Festschrift G. Ritter* (Tübingen, 1950), pp. 189 f.

that Urban Rhegius, the senior preacher at Augsburg before 1530, "converted" to Zwinglianism since as long as he had taught as a Lutheran, his church had been virtually empty.[13] When he emigrated to Lüneburg in 1531, of course he returned to Lutheranism.[14] Johannes Forster complained bitterly that the Augsburgers were all fanatics.[15] However, at Memmingen, Kempten, and Strasbourg, the Lutherans also carried on lonely struggles.[16] In the decades that followed, the sympathies of the people remained with the "Reformed" preachers. Even in the city of Ravensburg, which did not join the Reformation until the mid-1540s, the common man "preferred Zwinglianism to Lutheranism."[17] As late as 1559 Ravensburg dismissed the Lutheran Mehlhorn,[18] whose tenure at Augsburg four years earlier had also been cut short by congregational pressure, despite appointment by the Augsburg Council itself.[19] At Ulm there were citizens even in the seventeenth century who refused to take communion in the strict Lutheran city.[20]

13. F. Roth, *Augsburgs Reformationsgeschichte,* 2nd ed. (Munich, 1901–1911), 1:206.

14. On the inner development of Rhegius, to which the external change of parties corresponds, see O. Seitz, "Die theologische Entwicklung des Urbanus Rhegius, speziell sein Verhältnis zu Luther und zu Zwingli" (Diss., Halle, 1898); idem, "Die Stellung des Urbanus Rhegius im Abendmahlsstreit," *Zeitschrift für Kirchengeschichte* 19 (1899): 293–328.

15. F. Heer, "Augsburger Bürgertum im Aufstieg Augsburgs zur Weltstadt," in *Augusta, 955–1955* (Augsburg, 1955), p. 135.

16. For Memmingen, see F. Dobel, *Memmingen im Reformationszeitalter nach handschriftlichen und gleichzeitigen Quellen* (Augsburg, 1877), 2:68. On the great conflict at Kempten over the Supper, a conflict which ended in 1533 with the expulsion of the Lutheran preachers, see W. Köhler, *Zwingli und Luther* (Leipzig, 1924–1953), 2:315 ff.; O. Erhard, *Die Reformation der Kirche in Kempten auf Grund archivalischer Studien dargestellt* (Kempten, 1917), pp. 26 ff. For Strasbourg, see J. W. Baum, *Capito und Butzer* (Elberfeld, 1860), p. 339.

17. H. Günther, *Gerwig Blarer, Briefe und Akten* (Stuttgart, 1914–1921), p. 553.

18. G. Holzer, "Der Streit der Konfessionen in der Reichsstadt Ravensburg" (Diss., Tübingen, 1951), pp. 55 ff.

19. F. Roth, *Augsburgs Reformationsgeschichte,* 4:587. On the Augsburg disputes in the 1550s in which despite the magistrates' efforts at moderation the populace succeeded for the third time in imposing their will on the Lutherans, see ibid., pp. 578 ff.

20. F. Fritz, *Ulmische Kirchengeschichte vom Interim bis zum dreissigjährigen Krieg* (Stuttgart, 1934), pp. 152 ff.

If one asks which "Reformed" teachings aroused particular enthusiasm, we would have to rank the doctrine of communion first.[21] It is also worth noting, however, that in Kempten in 1533 a poll of the populace concerning the retention or elimination of images revealed eight hundred citizens against and only one hundred seventy-four in favor of retaining the "idols."[22] In 1549 the Ulm reformer Martin Frecht, then in exile, recommended to the city council that for political reasons it should introduce the Lutheran Nuremberg service, but at the same time he anxiously observed that the common man would certainly be repulsed by the Nuremberg "mass" and would ridicule it and declare it popish.[23]

2.

How can one explain both the remarkable division between the Protestant imperial cities and the deep roots of the "Reformed" doctrine in Upper Germany? First we must take into account a series of external factors. It is quite natural that cities of the same region, already quite closely united by common interests, should also be united on the issue of the Reformation and that when a few leading cities had chosen their course, other and smaller cities followed their lead.[24] Nevertheless, actual political considerations never played a decisive role. From the very beginning it was al-

21. Already in 1526 a Lutheran reported that the number of communicants increased when the Supper was celebrated in accord with Zwingli's doctrine. Köhler, *Zwingli und Luther,* 1:244. Philipp Ulhart, the Augsburg printer, switched in 1525 (the beginning of the controversy over the Supper) suddenly from printing texts by Luther to publishing polemical tracts against the communion doctrine of Wittenberg. K. Schottenloher, *Philipp Ulhart* (Freising, 1921), pp. 27 f. According to W. Köhler, who expresses this opinion repeatedly (e.g., *Huldrych Zwingli,* 2nd ed. [Stuttgart, 1952], p. 181), Zwingli's stubbornness in the negotiations, for example, at Marburg cannot ultimately be reduced to the fact that he would have been reproached in Zurich for any "Lutheran" changes in the Supper. It is difficult to see why the Zwinglian Supper had such an attraction.

22. Erhard, *Kempten,* p. 37.

23. Fritz, *Ulmische Kirchengeschichte,* p. 19. In fact, the council could not establish the Lutheran service in the 1550s. Ibid., pp. 45 ff.; Waldenmaier, *Gottesdienstordnungen,* p. 113.

24. It is characteristic that the Heilbronn reformer, the Lutheran Lachmann, had to warn his council against such considerations. Cf. M. von Rauch, *Urkunden der Stadt Heilbronn* (Stuttgart, 1922), vol. 4, no. 3237.

ways politically much more dangerous and delicate to choose Zwinglianism than to choose Lutheranism. In defending themselves against the great Catholic powers of southern Germany, however, only those cities in the immediate vicinity of Switzerland could really seek allies among the Protestant Swiss rather than among the distant North German Protestants, and even for them the possibility existed only in the years before the catastrophe at Kappel [in 1531]. In fact, for several years Strasbourg and Constance did form a "Christian Cities Pact" with the Swiss. But from 1531 on political considerations everywhere must have operated conclusively in favor of Luther since the Swiss had lost their political importance. Anyone wishing to conclude an alliance with the North Germans, however, would have to agree with their confession of faith.

Even more importantly, in the cities where the Reformation came first, the leading theologians and politicians felt that they had a missionary responsibility toward their sister cities. Thus, nonnative theologians, and especially Ambrosius Blaurer and Bucer, were responsible for the final organizational establishment of the Reformation in several of these imperial cities of southwestern Germany. Zwingli too had watched the spread of the Reformation in the imperial cities with unflagging attention and had encouraged it through a series of official letters to the councils of these cities.[25] Yet the Lutheran imperial cities also benefitted in the same way from the influence of one city on another. If, in the context of our study, we have to neglect the organizational activities of Bugenhagen and Amsdorff in the North German cities, we should not

---

25. Two of these are particularly interesting. First, the letter to Ulm of 27 April 1527 (*ZW-CR* 9, no. 606). It almost seems that Zwingli himself was aware of the urban character of his theology. The second document important for this study is Zwingli's introduction to his commentary on Jeremiah of 1531. He addressed this introduction to the council and community of Strasbourg (*ZW-CR* 14:417 ff.) as he had addressed his Introduction to Isaiah to the first of the cities with feudal rights (see above, part III, note 80). In this introduction he enthusiastically describes his ideal Christian city in which *magistratus* and *propheta* work together and he sees this ideal realized in Strasbourg (Ibid., p. 427, lines 17 ff.). One can easily imagine that these letters, which were so attuned to the urban mentality, had remarkable propaganda effect.

fail to mention Brenz, who carried on a lively propaganda campaign in southern Germany.[26]

The deeper reasons for the division of the imperial cities becomes more apparent when we observe that the Zwinglian cities also differed in other respects from the remaining imperial cities. For one thing, one must realize that North and South Germany were remarkably different from each other in the period just prior to the Reformation. On the one hand, this was clearly true for *social* and *economic* life. The decline of the Hanseatic League in northern Germany had fostered much sharper social conflicts than the economic depression which can also be observed in most of the cities of Upper Germany from the beginning of the sixteenth century. On the other hand, *intellectual* life was much less intense in the cities of northern Germany than in those of the South. When we said earlier that at the end of the Middle Ages the imperial cities were the real centers of culture in Germany, that applied strictly only to the South German cities. If we take the breadth of education as a standard, we find that the intellectual and cultural center of gravity before 1550 lay clearly in the South. The extremely timid beginnings of humanism in the cities of the North at the beginning of the sixteenth century provide a good indication of this.[27]

26. In Heilbronn, for example, in 1531. Cf. Rauch, *Heilbronn*, vol. 4, no. 3414e. Also in Reutlingen after 1527. Cf. Hartmann, *Matthäus Alber*, p. 104. See also, outside the circle of imperial cities the report on Crailsheim by J. Fischer, "Die Pfarrei Crailsheim im Mittelalter," *Württembergisch Franken* 41 (1957): 62. We also know that in 1527 Nuremberg tried to persuade the city of Ulm to dismiss its preacher, Sam, a disciple of Zwingli. T. Keim, *Die Reformation der Reichsstadt Ulm* (Stuttgart, 1851), p. 139. These events should sometime be studied more closely. See in the meantime F. W. Kantzenbach, "Johannes Brenz und die Reformation in Franken," *Zeitschrift für bayerische Kirchengeschichte* 31 (1962): 149–68.

27. M. E. Schlichting, "Religiöse und gesellschaftliche Anschauungen in den Hansestädten des späten Mittelalters" (Diss., Berlin, 1935), pp. 96 f. Similarly W. Andreas, "Die Kulturbedeutung der deutschen Reichsstadt zu Ausgang des Mittelalters," *Deutsche Vierteljahrsschrift für Literaturwissenschaft und Geistesgeschichte* 6 (1928): 105; idem, *Deutschland vor der Reformation*, 6th ed. (Stuttgart, 1959), p. 388. E. Spitta ("Haltung und Gesichtskreis des niederdeutschen Bürgers im 15. und 16. Jahrhundert," *Niedersächsisches Jahrbuch für Landesgeschichte* 16 [1939]: 138 ff.) maintains that only at the end of the sixteenth century did the burghers of Hildesheim become aware of humanism. A work such as that by Schlichting suggests that religious conflicts in the Hanseatic cities were relatively insignificant. Still, it is difficult to find a standard to judge this.

For these reasons, the introduction of the Reformation into the free cities of northern Germany was accompanied nearly everywhere by social unrest in much greater degree than in southern Germany; but at the same time the ecclesiastical changeover happened less tempestuously and passionately. The North German cities did not produce any independent theologian of great stature; instead they allowed their Reformation to be organized by Wittenberg through such men as Bugenhagen or Amsdorf. And the people there were much less disposed to religious radicalism than in the South. Of course, occasional iconoclasm occurred in the North, as in Hamburg or in Brunswick.[28] But the ideas of Zwingli did not penetrate very deeply,[29] nor could sectarianism spread nearly so well as in Strasbourg, Augsburg, or Regensburg.[30] The North German cities were spiritually and intellectually much less disposed to the Reformation than were those in the South.[31] Thus the Reformation proceeded there more conservatively.

Even though the "Reformed" and the Lutheran cities of the South were alike in being socially, culturally, and spiritually different from the cities of the North, from another point of view they also exhibit very marked and basic differences among them-

28. K. Beckey, *Die Reformation in Hamburg* (Hamburg, 1929), p. 149; Lau, "Der Bauernkrieg," p. 123.

29. See, however, note 42 of this part.

30. On the penetration of the Anabaptists into the cities on the Baltic Sea, see J. Schildhauer, *Soziale, politische und religiöse Auseinandersetzungen in den Hansestädten Stralsund, Rostock und Wismar im ersten Drittel des 16. Jahrhundert* (Weimar, 1959), pp. 162, 170. The beautiful book by D. Cantimori, *Italienische Häretiker der Spätrenaissance* (Basel, 1949), (see also the reviews by H. Bornkamm, *Historische Zeitschrift* 182 [1956]: 183 f., and G. Ritter, *Archiv für Reformationsgeschichte* 37 [1940]: 268–89) makes it stimulatingly clear how much attraction the free cities of South Germany and Switzerland had for the Italian refugees. But, unless I am wrong, not one of these refugees settled down in a city of North Germany.

31. To realize how much the cities of Southwest Germany had been prepared for the Reformation one need just consider the characterization of the Pope as Antichrist, a notion that Luther had to struggle with but which flowed easily from the pen of Sebastian Brant. W. Köhler, "Humanismus und Reformation im Elsass," in *Deutsches Schicksal im Elsass* (1941), p. 72. G. W. Locher, "Das Geschichtsbild Huldrych Zwinglis," *Theologische Zeitschrift* 9 (1953): 294, remarks that even Zwingli had no inhibitions in this respect and did not surprise his listeners.

selves.[32] We have already briefly mentioned that Luther's teachings were dominant in Franconia and Bucer's and Zwingli's in Swabia. In fact, the ancient folk-boundary between the Franconian and Swabian imperial cities coincided with the boundary separating the two Protestant parties. Augsburg and Esslingen are not only the first Swabian cities in the North and East, but also the first to have rallied to Bucer. At the same time the Swabian burghers were linked to the Alemannic towns of Alsace and Switzerland not only in their type of Reformation but by ties of ethnic kinship.[33]

There was a second difference between the Lutheran and "Reformed" cities, related to the first, but actually more important for the course of the Reformation. More than just an ethnic frontier separated Heilbronn from Esslingen or Donauwörth from

32. This fact indicates decisively how H. Köditz repeatedly leapt to conclusions in her article "Die gesellschaftlichen Ursachen des Scheiterns des Marburger Religionsgesprächs," *Zeitschrift für Geschichtswissenschaft* 2 (1954): 37–70. This essay is a classic example of a priori history. It can be seen from the outset that the author worked completely from secondary literature but nevertheless did not even know the basic monograph on her topic, the 1929 book by W. Köhler, *Das Marburger Religionsgespräch 1529, Versuch einer Rekonstruktion* (Leipzig, 1929), and disposed of all challenges by liberal quotations from Marx and Engels. The oppressive, dogmatic narrowness of the result is commensurate with the method: union was impossible at Marburg because the "ideologue of princely absolutism based upon territorial possessions" (Luther) and the representative of the "progressive bourgeois conviction" of the "Swiss middle class" (Zwingli) came together, and the difference in the conception of communion (the passivism and mysticism of Luther versus the activism and rationalism of Zwingli) was generated by this classic opposition. Naturally, when considered closely, even Zwingli was reactionary, since he too still used religion as a "cloak for political and social aspirations." If this were correct as stated, then there would be no way to understand why Nuremberg, for example, did not adopt Zwinglianism as did Zurich since the two cities do not differ essentially in their social structure or their "progressive bourgeois conviction." And the fact that Zwinglianism existed in Nuremberg but was repressed cannot be simply explained by saying that the ruling burghers, divided between their conviction and their lust for domination, decided for the latter and thereby for ecclesiastical compromise (that is, for Lutheranism). This assumption contradicts, for example, the history of the Reformation in Strasbourg (see on this point note 39 of this part). If one frees it of its conceptual simplifications and rejects its inflexible linkage of economic substructure and theological consequences, Köditz's exposition would have its flashes of truth. But in its present form it is unacceptable.
33. The fourteen signators of the so-called Swabian Syngramma, a polemic concerning the Supper published in 1526 and directed against Oecolampadius, were not, properly speaking, pastors of Swabian congregations but rather of Franconian congregations.

Augsburg. For in the Franconian free cities as in the free cities of northern Germany, the lower classes of the population were almost completely cut off from direct participation in the government of their city.[34] Some cities, like Nuremberg, had patrician governments guaranteed by constitutions.[35] In others the custom of excluding the guilds from government had become common law during the fifteenth century, as in Heilbronn.[36] This state of affairs appears particularly significant in that one often encounters in Franconian cities a certain apathy among the people toward communal affairs and a certain alienation from the communal idea.[37] This does not seem to be the case in the Swabian and Alemannic regions.[38] Still we must not forget that here too in the course of

34. On this difference between South and North Germany see above, part I, notes 3 and 9. W. Ebel (*Der Bürgereid als Geltungsgrund und Gestaltungsprinzip des deutschen mittelalterlichen Stadtrechts* [Weimar, 1958], p. 22) maintains that in the northern Germany of the late Middle Ages it appears that "the *communio iurata* of the citizenry was attenuated past recognition." In the Reformation period the Franconian city of Schwäbisch Hall was an exception. From 1512 the artisans there were even the [ruling] majority. G. Wunder, "Die Ratsherren der Reichsstadt Hall, 1487–1803," *Württembergisch Franken* 46 (1962): 107.

35. This was noticed by the Venetian ambassador at the Imperial Diet of 1543: "Nuremberg, contrary to the custom of all the other cities of Germany, is governed by nobility." Quoted by E. Franz, *Nürnberg, Kaiser und Reich* (Munich, 1930), p. 156.

36. A. Schlitz, "Verfassung und Verwaltung der Reichsstadt Heilbronn im Mittelalter" (Diss., Tübingen, 1911), p. 85.

37. Characteristic of this situation is the complaint made by the leader of the Schweinfurt revolt that he had been abandoned by the very community he had wished to help. F. Stein, *Geschichte der Reichsstadt Schweinfurt* (Schweinfurt, 1900), p. 105. And this complaint was repeated in Regensburg during the Reformation. L. Theobald, *Die Reformationsgeschichte der Reichsstadt Regensburg* (Munich, 1936), 1:116. In Schwäbisch Gmünd there were many reports as early as 1488, as well as later during the Reformation period, of the lively efforts of the artisans to shirk governmental office. E. Naujoks, *Obrigkeitsgedanke, Zunftverfassung und Reformation. Studien zur Geschichte von Ulm, Esslingen und Schwäbisch Gmünd* (Stuttgart, 1958), pp. 22, 41, 97, 101. This desire was also expressed at Memmingen in 1544. E. Maschke, "Verfassung und soziale Kräfte in der deutschen Stadt des späten Mittelalters, vornehmlich in Oberdeutschland," *Vierteljahrschrift für Sozial- und Wirtschaftsgeschichte* 46 (1959): 439, n. 410. The comment in the article by H. Spitzer, "Zur geschichte des Reformationsstreites zwischen Hamburg und dem Domkapitel," *Mitteilungen des Vereins für Hamburgische Geschichte* 9 (1908): 18, n. 1, on Bucer's "Advice to Hamburg" in 1545 is instructive concerning the difference in thought between a northern and southern German burgher.

38. In general see H. Planitz, *Die deutsche Stadt im Mittelalter* (Cologne and Graz, 1954), pp. 326 f.

the fifteenth century the achievements of the guild struggles were not fully maintained. Yet in the sixteenth century, so far as I know, there was no Swabian city in which the guilds did not play a decisive role in government. And even if this privileged constitutional position of the guilds did not necessarily mean that the artisans were absolute lords of the city,[39] nonetheless during the Reformation of the Upper German cities, the lower classes of the populace clearly had a strong influence on and interest in the city government. Moreover, K. S. Bader[40] has shown in a larger context that the communal idea in the late Middle Ages already constituted the fundamental element of constitutional development in all the southwestern German-speaking territories. It was this communal idea which bound the Alemannic and Swabian region together. If, however, this much is correct, we can make an additional observation. Although the Swiss were effectively separated from the empire after the Swabian War [1499–1500], we can say that when the Upper German cities adopted the Zwinglian Reformation, they once again overcame this separation, if not in a legal at least in a spiritual sense.

These peculiarities of constitutional structure and thought clearly played a more important role in the success of Zwingli and Bucer than did ethnic differences. The occasional sympathies for "Reformed" doctrines in the cities of central and northern Germany as far north as Lübeck and Rostock make this point clear.[41] But

---

39. See above, part I, note 5. Even, for example, in the complex governmental system of Strasbourg (cf. on this point U. Crämer, *Die Verfassung und Verwaltung Strassburgs von der Reformationszeit bis zum Fall der Reichsstadt, 1512 bis 1681* [Frankfurt a. M., 1931]) the patrician element was stronger than the guild element.

40. See above, part I, note 35.

41. Especially in Nuremberg where the council in 1525–26 was able to stave off Zwinglianism only by the most energetic efforts (proscribing the writings of Luther's opponents, prohibiting discussions on the Lord's Supper in inns, and so on). See on this point F. Roth, *Einführung der Reformation in Nürnberg* (Würzburg, 1885), pp. 225 ff.; A. Engelhardt, *Die Reformation in Nürnberg* (Nuremberg, 1937), 2:48 ff.; W. Köhler, *Zwingli und Luther*, 1:229 f. Someone should make a detailed study of the early North German Zwinglianism, which was occasionally mixed with Anabaptism and which was widespread especially among the lower classes.

no imperial city outside of Upper Germany allowed these sympathies to lead to a "Reformed" victory.[42]

Of course, many contemporaries were convinced that a connection existed between the constitutional structure and the "Reformed" Protestant movement. A characteristic example is the request of 1547/48 addressed by the patricians of Augsburg to Charles V, in which they asked for a modification of the constitution of Augsburg, taking Nuremberg as a model:

> . . . on the other hand, in the city Nuremberg, where the honorable families hold power and carry the responsibility, one sees a much better administration and a much greater discretion in spiritual affairs and temporal policies than where the rabble rule and have the upper hand, that is a *much milder and more tolerable form of religious Reformation, whose form retains many Christian ceremonies* . . . and therefore a worthy example to follow. The city Nuremberg candidly acknowledges how much store is set on the fact that the honorable families should rule and not the ignorant rabble. Indeed, the community itself (if it had the power and the choice) would clearly have been entirely disposed to rally to the rebels in open revolt, no less than the other towns that are imperial cities (i.e., in the Schmalkaldic War). But, thanks to the fact that the magistracy there was held by honorable families, Nuremberg was preserved from such a catastrophe. And while all the other cities in which the rabble is powerful have defected, she alone has remained in obedience, peace, and tranquillity.[43]

We have seen that the cities which were best organized according to the communal principle and most conscious of this organization were precisely those which Zwingli and Bucer conquered. If this conclusion is correct, we see in it the strongest confirmation of our thesis that the theology of these two founders of the "Reformed" tradition was decisively influenced at important points by the very

42. At the most we could name Frankfurt am Main and Worms, both of whose ecclesiastics adhered to Zwingli for a while. However, we could never consider the two cities as a whole to be "Reformed." See H. Dechent, *Kirchengeschichte von Frankfurt am Main seit der Reformation* (Frankfurt a. M., 1913), and A. Weckerling, *Leonhart Brunner, der erste vom Rate der Reichsstadt Worms angestellte evangelische Prediger* (Worms, 1895).
43. Quoted as in D. Langemantel, *Historie des Regiments in des Heiligen Römischen Reichs Stadt Augspurg* (Augsburg, 1734), p. 72. Cf. Zwingli's letter to Ulm quoted above in note 25 of this part.

existence and the peculiar mentality of the urban community where they worked.[44] The townsmen, when they manifested their passionate preference for the distinctive signs of the "Reformed" doctrine, by rejecting the real presence in the communion, by iconoclasm, by preferring simplification of divine service, showed how successful that doctrine was. At the same time, in adapting their message to the mentality and the life of the city, Zwingli, Bucer, and their followers[45] were capable of profoundly transforming the thought of the townsmen.

We have arrived at the following conclusion: *the victory of the "Reformed" Reformation in the Upper German imperial cities is finally explained by the encounter of the peculiarly "urban" theology of Zwingli and Bucer with the particularly vital communal spirit in Upper Germany.*

V. THE DECLINE OF THE FREE CITIES

1.

Under the spiritual direction of Martin Bucer, the tide of Zwinglianism reached its high point in the imperial cities in the 1530s. This tide began to ebb as soon as the initial enthusiasm for the Reformation subsided. The Reformation surge in communal thinking declined as well. A whole series of factors was responsible for this development.

In general, the imperial cities had seriously compromised their political situation by adopting the Reformation. They had alienated

44. There is hardly any South German evidence that the "Reformed" theologians ever urged their listeners to go beyond their communal tendencies to specifically revolutionary social demands of the sort that Schildhauer, *Auseinandersetzungen in den Hansestädten,* seems to have found in the coastal cities of Mecklenburg and Hither Pomerania (pp. 161 ff.). For Zurich, see the evidence in the article by N. Birnbaum, "The Zwinglian Reformation in Zurich," *Archive de Sociologie des Religions* 8 (1959): 15–30. According to Wunder ("Ratsherren der Reichsstadt Hall," p. 117) we have no evidence that any compromise on social issues between supporters and opponents of the Reformation was necessary in Schwäbisch Hall.

45. In my work on the Reformation at Constance I tried to show how greatly the urban mentality influenced the theology and ecclesiastical activity of the local reformers. The beautiful New Year's song by J. Zwick, the reformer of Constance, "Nun wölle Gott, das unser gsang" furnishes an example of this influence accessible to all.

themselves from the emperor and the empire,[1] causing a change in their self-image,[2] and the sixteenth century saw stirring attempts by imperial cities to reconcile their Protestantism with their fidelity to the empire.[3] In addition, by alienating themselves from the emperor, the cities weakened their position in regard to the princely states that threatened their existence. The Habsburgs themselves now intervened as an occupying power, unsuccessfully with regard to the cities in Middle Baden [Offenburg, Gengenbach, Zell am Harmersbach] but successfully in the case of Constance. Political considerations even led some cities to remain at least temporarily faithful to Catholicism. The two imperial cities of Thuringia, for example, carried on a desperate struggle after the Peasants' War to remain independent from the neighboring Protestant princes and clearly sought the support of the emperor

1. To be sure, this alienation began as early as the fifteenth century. H. Schmidt, *Die deutschen Städtechroniken als Spiegel des bürgerlichen Selbstverständnisses im Spätmittelalter* (Göttingen, 1958), p. 42. H. Baron in his "Religion and Politics in the German Imperial Cities during the Reformation" (*English Historical Review* 52 [1937]: 405–27, 614–33) summarizes the political history of the Protestant imperial cities during the Reformation and finds in the first years of the reign of Charles V a number of attempts at collaboration between cities and emperor against the territorial princes. But these hopeful movements soon fell apart, and they disappeared altogether after the Protestation of Speyer (1529).
2. The book by H. Schmidt, *Städtechroniken*, proves how strongly the burghers of imperial cities were still bound to the empire in the fifteenth century, and how thoroughly this bond influenced their thought.
3. According to E. Franz, *Nürnberg, Kaiser und Reich* (Munich, 1930), loyalty to the empire was the primary motive for the peculiarly vacillating policies of Nuremberg in the 1530s and 1540s. On the causes of this attitude, see also Baron, "Religion and Politics," p. 614. In adopting the Reformation in 1528, Goslar explicitly reserved obedience to the emperor and the empire. U. Hölscher, *Die Geschichte der Reformation in Goslar* (Hannover, 1902), p. 33. In addition, in the sixteenth century one finds it commonly said that if God's will and the will of the emperor were opposed, one had to follow God alone. In the mouth of a burgher of an imperial city, such words were not spoken lightly. Yet it is necessary to take seriously (as does F. Rörig, *Die europäische Stadt und die Kultur des Bürgertums im Mitteralter* [Göttingen, 1955]) the protestations of loyalty in the well-known *Instruction* of Strasbourg to the emperor in 1552, in which the city asked for aid against the French and stressed its loyalty to the empire. *Politische Correspondenz der Stadt Strassburg im Zeitalter der Reformation,* Urkunden und Akten der Stadt Strassburgs, 2nd section, vol. 5 (Strasbourg, 1882–1928/33), no. 288, especially pp. 386 f. This seems doubtful to me on the basis of statements by other persons from Strasbourg (for example, see note 10 below). Moreover, one could assert that in the cities on the edge of the empire (the cities of the Hanse, in Lorraine, and in Switzerland) the feeling of loyalty to the empire was declining.

by maintaining a sincere, or at least external, fidelity to the old church.[4] The political motive is even more clear in the history of the Reformation in Rottweil. When King Ferdinand threatened in 1529 that he would remove his Superior Court of Justice if the town accepted the Reformation, Rottweil promptly suppressed a strong Protestant congregation and expelled around four hundred citizens.[5] It is noteworthy that even the citizens, at least in this case, showed a certain disposition to support the policy of their councils.[6]

To be sure, the political rupture between the Protestant cities and the empire was neutralized when the cities and the Protestant princes came together in a common faith and united in the Schmalkaldic League.[7] But beginning in 1540 difficulties piled up.

4. See the works of G. Schmidt, "Die Reformation in Nordhausen" (Diss., Göttingen, 1924), and H. Nebelsieck, "Reformationsgeschichte der Stadt Mühlhausen in Thüringen," *Zeitschrift des Vereins für Kirchengeschichte in der Provinz Sachsen* 1 (1904): 59–115, 208–56; 2 (1904): 48–120, 159–227. The same situation probably prevailed in Weilderstadt in Swabia. *Beschreibung des Oberamts Leonberg*, 2nd ed. (Stuttgart, 1923), p. 1079.
5. On this point see J. Speh, "Beiträge zur Reformationsgeschichte des oberen Neckargebietes" (Diss., Tübingen, 1920); F. Thudichum, *Geschichte der Reichsstadt Rottweil und des Kaiserlichen Hofgerichts daselbst* (Tübingen, 1911), pp. 44 ff.
6. For the Thuringian cities see above, part II, note 16. Nevertheless, in 1551 the populace of Nordhausen finally rebelled against the policy of their city secretary, Meyenburg. G. Schmidt, "Nordhausen," pp. 54 ff. Even in Rottweil there were reported signs that members of the community sympathized (although timidly) with the Catholic council (Speh, "Reformationsgeschichte des oberen Neckargebietes," pp. 26 ff.), a fact worth noting since it is without parallel. In fact, loyalty to Catholicism was well rewarded. Thus as early as 1528 Überlingen received an improved coat of arms as reward for its perseverance "in the last Lutheran and peasant revolt and in the serious problems of insurrection." Ç. Roder, "Zur Lebensgeschichte des Pfarrers Dr. Johannes Schlupf in Überlingen," *Freiburger Diözesan-Archiv*, n.s. 16 (1915): 283. A year later the emperor announced that he would undertake the payment of half of the city's imperial tax. J. Kühn, *Die Geschichte des Speyer Reichstag 1529* (Leipzig, 1929), p. 247. In 1530 Rottweil was relieved of tax payments for a fifteen-year period. Speh, "Reformationsgeschichte des oberen Neckargebietes," p. 44. In the same year Donauwörth received the right to coin money as a reward for its loyalty to Catholicism. M. Zelzer, *Geschichte der Stadt Donauwörth* (Donauwörth, 1958), p. 175. Cologne, Nordhausen, Weilderstadt, and surely many other cities received similar rewards. L. Ennen, *Geschichte der Stadt Coeln* (Cologne, 1875), p. 447; G. Schmidt, "Nordhausen," p. 45; *Beschreibung des Oberamts Leonburg*, p. 1080.
7. In 1526 the first alliance planned by Philip of Hesse was shattered by, among other things, the lack of trust between the cities and princes. F. Roth, *Augsburgs Reformationsgeschichte*, 2nd ed. (Munich, 1901–1911),

First, with the Diet of Speyer in 1542, open conflict broke out again concerning the right of the cities to cast an equal vote at the diet, a matter that touched directly the legal guarantee of their freedom.[8] In addition, the solidarity between princes and cities in the Schmalkaldic League began to weaken.[9]

This development forced the cities once again to strengthen the authority of their governments. In addition, the more realistic city magistrates dealing with foreign affairs began once more to put politics ahead of theology. Regardless of confessional differences, they promoted the idea of reviving the old community of interests of all the imperial cities.[10] Similarly the Upper German disdain for a general theological *rapprochement* with Lutheranism disappeared, especially since certain obstacles had been cleared away by the theologians after the Diet of Augsburg in 1530.[11] To be sure, the Lutheranism of the South Germans in the 1530s was generally not very profound; the comment of Forster describes the situation well: "They put on the Saxon Confession only as a

---

1:274; Baron, "Religion and Politics," pp. 410 ff. E. Franz remarks that around 1530 there was a very unusual harmony between Nuremberg and Brandenburg-Ansbach, which, of course, did not last long. Franz, *Nürnberg, Kaiser und Reich*, pp. 119, 127.

8. See on this subject the article by H. Gerber, "Die Bedeutung des Augsburger Reichstages von 1547/48 für das Ringen der Reichsstädte um Stimme, Stand und Session," *Elsässisch-Lothringisches Jahrbuch* 9 (1930): 168–208; M. Huber, "Städtearchiv und Reichsstandschaft der Städte im 16. Jahrhundert," *Ulm und Oberschwaben* 35 (1958): 94–112. Cf. also E. Naujoks, *Obrigkeitsgedanke, Zunftverfassung und Reformation. Studien zur Geschichte von Ulm, Esslingen und Schwäbisch Gmünd* (Stuttgart, 1958), pp. 103 ff.

9. Especially after the Brunswick War. Cf. Roth, *Augsburgs Reformationsgeschichte*, pp. 3, 70, 77. Still, as early as the founding of the League, there were tensions between cities and princes. See E. Fabian, *Die Entstehung des Schmalkaldischen Bundes und seiner Verfassung 1529–31/33* (Tübingen, 1956), pp. 89 f., 101 ff., 125 f.

10. In 1542 the Strasbourg citizen Kniebis proposed in Basel an alliance against the princes, the "furious wolves," who were less to be trusted than the Turks. He wished to include the [Swiss] confederates "regardless of which religion they belonged to"; *Politische Correspondenz* 3, no. 290. Cf. ibid., no. 297, where "mainly those of our religion" are mentioned as possible allies. In the Imperial Diets after 1542, the Catholic cities, led by Cologne, united with the Protestants on the issue of city participation in the diet.

11. For this subject, see the second volume of W. Köhler, *Zwingli und Luther*, 2 vols. (Leipzig, 1924–1953), as well as E. Bizer, *Studien zur Geschichte des Abenmahlsstreits im 16. Jahrhundert*, 2nd ed. (Darmstadt, 1962).

breastplate."[12] After the beginning of the 1540s, the imperial cities of Upper Germany began here and there to trust pastoral charges to declared partisans of Luther. When in 1543 Isny installed Johann Marbach, whom Luther himself had promoted to the rank of doctor, people still spoke of it as the *scandalum Isnense*,[13] but already in 1545 the same Marbach went unopposed to occupy a chair in Strasbourg. In the same year, Matthias Rot, another immediate disciple of Luther, became pastor at Lindau.[14]

The crisis years between 1547 and 1555 were decisive in the decline of the old order in Upper Germany. While some of the Protestant Franconian cities remained neutral in the Schmalkaldic War,[15] despite the occasionally violent opposition of their citizens, almost all their sisters of Swabia and Alsace took part[16] and had to bear the principal burden of the war in South Germany. They had to make enormous expenditures for war taxes and maintenance of the army before the defeat and had to pay heavy punitive taxes thereafter.[17] The same situation emerged five years later at the time of the campaign of Maurice of Saxony in southern

12. Quoted by Bizer, *Geschichte des Abenmahlsstreits*, p. 136.

13. T. Schiess, *Briefwechsel der Brüder Ambrosius und Thomas Blaurer* (Freiburg i.B., 1908–1910), vol. 2, no. 1235; I. Kammerer, "Die Reformation in Isny," *Zeitschrift für bayerische Kirchengeschichte* 53 (1953): 37 ff. As early as 1536/37 the Zwinglian Algesheimer was replaced in Frankfurt by Peter Geltner, a passionate Lutheran. H. Dechent, *Kirchengeschichte von Frankfurt am Main seit der Reformation* (Frankfurt a. M., 1913), pp. 149 f.

14. K. Wolfart, *Geschichte der Stadt Lindau am Bodensee* (Lindau, 1909), p. 315.

15. For example, Nuremberg. Cf. E. Franz, *Nürnberg, Kaiser und Reich*, pp. 172 f. Nuremberg never joined the Schmalkaldic League and other Franconian cities only joined late. In each instance this caution was in large part based on Luther's opinion that one did not have the right to resist the emperor, an opinion that Luther himself no longer held strongly after 1529. K. Müller, *Luthers Äusserungen über das Recht des bewaffneten Widerstandes gegen den Kaiser*, Sitzungsberichte der bayr. Akad. der Wissenschaften, phil.-hist. Klasse (Munich, 1915), pp. 28 f. For other reasons see Baron, "Religion and Politics," p. 422. As for Heilbronn, see M. Duncker, "Heilbronn zur Zeit des Schmalkaldischen Kriegs und des Interims" (Diss., Tübingen, 1904), p. 3. See also note 3 in this part.

16. Kaufbeuren remained aloof. See K. Alt, *Reformation und Gegenreformation in der freien Reichsstadt Kaufbeuren* (Munich, 1932), p. 84.

17. F. W. Schaafhausen, "Die Geldwirtschaft des schmalkaldischen Bundes" (Diss., Göttingen, 1921), pp. 93 ff.; H. Gerber, "Die Kriegsrechnungen des schmalkaldischen Bundes über den Krieg im Oberland des Jahres 1546," *Archiv für Reformationsgeschichte* 32 (1935): 41–93, 218–47; 33 (1936): 226–35; 34 (1937): 87–122, 272–88.

Germany. Probably none of the cities was able to recover entirely from such serious financial damages. Furthermore, this whole region, in contrast to northern Germany, had to accept the Interim at least formally[18] and with it elements completely foreign to the cities; new church ordinances, for example, were imposed on them by outside force. The divisions among the townsmen were also perpetuated by the Peace of Augsburg which contained an article calling for "Simultaneity" [i.e., toleration of both Catholics and Protestants].[19] This too was entirely alien to the mentality of the city.

The hardest blow sustained by the old order, however, came from a different direction.[20] When the victorious emperor concluded that guild participation in the city government was responsible for the Reformation in the Upper German cities,[21] he abolished the constitutions of twenty-eight cities[22] between 1548

---

18. There was probably no Protestant imperial city in which the Interim did not meet with resistance from the population. Proof of this can be found nearly everywhere.

19. To be sure, it was only effective in a few cities of Upper Germany. On this subject see G. Pfeiffer, "Der Augsburger Religionsfrieden und die Reichsstädte," *Zeitschrift des historischen Vereins für Schwaben* 61 (1955): especially pp. 278 ff., as well as W. Friedensburg, "Das Protokoll der auf dem Augsburger Reichstage von 1555 versammelten Vertreter der freien und Reichsstädte über die Reichstagsverhandlungen," *Archiv für Reformationsgeschichte* 34 (1937): 36–86. Characteristically, the cities on which it was imposed always attacked this article by displaying a concern for peace and unity in the city, for example, as in Strasbourg (*Politische Correspondenz* 5, no. 507). This is the same argument that the cities had previously used to impose the new faith on everyone as soon as a majority of the citizenry had adopted it.

20. For that which follows see L. Fürstenwerth, "Die Verfassungsänderungen in den oberdeutschen Städten zur Zeit Karls V" (Diss., Göttingen, 1893); Naujoks, *Obrigkeitsgedanke*, pp. 118 ff.

21. The emperor came to this conclusion for various reasons. Cf. Fürstenwerth, "Verfassungsänderungen," p. 18, and the letter of the Abbot Gerwig Blarer, quoted by H. Günter, *Gerwig Blarer, Briefe und Akten*, 2 vols. (Stuttgart, 1914–1921), no. 1143.

22. In order to get a measure of uniformity, even Catholic cities were included as well as those Franconian cities which still had no aristocratic constitution. See the list in the work by Fürstenwerth, "Verfassungsänderungen," p. 37. In addition to this, like Augsburg and Ulm which had their "constitutional revolution" as early as 1548 (Ibid., pp. 20 ff.), Constance was also politically reorganized in the beginning of 1549, several months after its degradation to the status of an Austrian territorial city. See on this point A. Maurer, "Der Übergang der Stadt Konstanz an das Haus Österreich nach dem Schmalkaldischen Kriege," *Schriften des Vereins*

and 1552. In their place he established new ones which concentrated practically all power in the hands of the Small Council, which the people soon were calling "The Rabbit Council."[23] These self-perpetuating councils were composed almost exclusively of patricians who were members for life. Furthermore, all the guilds were dissolved. The official reason for this measure was that the poor artisans ought to be free of administrative burdens so that they might lead honorable lives and devote themselves exclusively to feeding their wives and children.[24] This explanation was not totally hypocritical, but the secret instructions which accompanied it revealed the true meaning: it was necessary to appoint such persons "who were closest to the ancient, true Christian religion."[25] The changes led to a situation in which it could be reported from Donauwörth, for example, that "several among the mayors and secret councillors could not read or write, but this did not disqualify them; rather they were found honest and upright and of the type more qualified than others for these offices."[26]

For a time townsmen in several locations put up an energetic passive resistance, and, at the time of the Princes' Revolt in the summer of 1552, several cities once again dismissed their "Rabbit Council" and reestablished the old constitution. But in the long run the imperial order prevailed. Soon the new members of the councils even received remuneration,[27] the city government took

---

für Geschichte des Bodensees und seiner Umgebung 33 (1904): 80. In contrast, Strasbourg and the other Alsatian imperial cities were spared. Elsewhere, the Catholic cities were treated much more accommodatingly than the Protestant cities (Überlingen, for example, was treated with "the true patience of a lamb"), and some were allowed in later years to reestablish their old order. Fürstenwerth, "Verfassungsänderungen," pp. 39, 100.

23. After the imperial commissioner Dr. Heinrich Hasse. [This is a play on words. "Hasse" is the man's name, "Hase" is a rabbit, and "Hass" means "hatred." Ed.]

24. Fürstenwerth, "Verfassungsänderungen," p. 33.

25. Ibid., p. 26. Cf. also p. 30.

26. Zelzer, *Donauwörth*, p. 198.

27. Fürstenwerth, "Verfassungsänderungen," pp. 94 f. Before this, the custom did not exist. H. Preuss, *Die Entwicklung des deutschen Städtewesens* (Leipzig, 1906), p. 85.

on an increasingly bureaucratic character,[28] and in most cases a small number of families took control.[29]

Thus the old urban community was systematically broken to pieces.[30] However, the principal goal of this action was to curtail the development of Protestantism in Upper Germany, which seems to prove the correctness of our line of argument. That goal was actually attained in places. In some cities, as for example in Biberach,[31] a small Catholic minority maintained a tyrannical rule for decades over a large Protestant majority. Elsewhere, the enforcement of the Interim for at least a few years assured the survival of a Catholic minority.

In all of the Protestant cities of Upper Germany, however, Lutheranism now took control of the church. This development was inevitable after 1555 when the [Lutheran] adherents of the Augsburg Confession received recognition in imperial law. Yet it is significant that the cities were no longer satisfied as before with a merely external conformity to the doctrine of the North Germans. At least the theologians and magistrates were now ready to draw more thoroughgoing conclusions in their efforts to conform. By 1553 Ulm had already officially abolished the ecclesiastical ordi-

28. This is emphasized by E. Naujoks, "Stadtverfassung und Ulmer Land im Zeitalter der Reformation," *Ulm und Oberschwaben* 34 (1955): 111, as well as by the instructive article by K. Bader, "Die Reichsstädte des schwäbischen Kreises am Ende des alten Reiches," *Ulm und Oberschwaben* 32 (1951): 47–70, which gives some particularly suggestive examples.

29. In Schwäbisch Hall after 1552, one could speak without circumlocutions of the right of inheritance of municipal offices. G. Wunder, "Die Ratsherren der Reichsstadt Hall, 1487–1803," *Württembergisch Franken* 46 (1962): 113.

30. To show how the times and opinions had changed, we will mention a characteristic episode cited by Fürstenwerth, "Verfassungsänderungen," p. 25: when the seventy-two members of the Small Council of Ulm appeared before Charles V in 1548, he is said to have exclaimed: "My God, what could so many do in a council? How could plain, simple people understand things of such importance?" It seems that it was little different in Augsburg. Naujoks, *Obrigkeitsgedanke*, p. 121.

31. For Biberach, cf. the instructive and copiously documented work by G. Pfeiffer, "Das Ringen um die Parität in der Reichsstadt Biberach," *Blätter für württembergische Kirchengeschichte* 56 (1956): 3–75. The numerical proportion seems to have been at first (1555) 6000:200; finally in 1635, before the establishment of parity in the Peace of Westphalia, there were approximately forty Catholics out of three hundred full citizens. Pfeiffer, "Biberach," pp. 13, 19, 57.

nance of 1531.[32] In 1561 Strasbourg withdrew from the *Tetra-politana*[33] and even tried to disavow its "Reformed" past. In 1556 Calvin was not allowed to preach during his visit to the city[34] although he still had many followers there. The Reformed community was soon suppressed in the same manner as Catholics and sectarians.[35] In 1598 when they added a historical introduction to the great church ordinance, they made it seem as if Strasbourg had been a faithful follower of the *Confessio Augustana* ever since 1531.[36] Everywhere cities gradually suppressed or restricted the lay positions of the church.[37] Slowly even pastors appointed by the magistracy[38] became city officials both in position and in the way they carried out their office. In 1562 Ambrosius Blaurer visited several cities in southern Swabia after a long asylum in Switzerland. In viewing those regions where he had been a major reformer just a generation earlier, he thought that he could tell that both clergy and magistrates, as well as the people, "had entirely ceased practicing their religion in that true and upright manner that they had used of old."[39]

32. F. Fritz, *Ulmische Kirchengeschichte vom Interim bis zum dreissig-jährigen Krieg* (Stuttgart, 1934), p. 43.

33. J. Adam, *Evangelische Kirchengeschichte der Stadt Strassburgs* (Strasbourg, 1928), p. 334.

34. Ibid, p. 327.

35. Ibid., p. 391.

36. Ibid., p. 358. One also finds there references to the reply by Beuther, preacher of Deux-Ponts.

37. For example, at Strasbourg: F. Wendel, *L'Eglise de Strasbourg. Sa constitution et son organization, 1532–1535* (Paris, 1942), p. 238; at Ulm: Fritz, *Ulmische Kirchengeschichte*, p. 58.

38. Of course, that also occurred in the "Reformed" period. Still these measures were justified by the idea that the council was the instrument of the urban community. Thus in 1545 in Bucer's "Advice to Hamburg," he characterized the church as a republic. H. von Schubert, "Die Beteiligung der dänisch-holsteinischen Landesfürsten am hamburgischen Kapitelstreit und das Gutachten Martin Bucers von 1545," *Schriften des Vereins für schleswig-holsteinische Kirchengeschichte* 2/3 (1904/05): 49.

39. Schiess, *Ambrosius und Thomas Blaurer*, nos. 2487 and 2489. Of course, a certain "Reformed" element was maintained in the cities of Upper Germany, in many places up to the present day. It is, for example, striking that in Strasbourg as well as in Ulm the Zwinglian austerity of liturgy and church ornamentation was maintained for a long time. Cf. Fritz, *Ulmische Kirchengeschichte*, pp. 160 ff.; C. Hallier, "Das Strassburger Kirchenwesen als Glied des deutschen Luthertums im 16. und 17. Jahrhundert," *Elsässisch-Lothring. Jahrbuch* 9 (1930): 222. Even in a book such as that by F.

Lutheranism was only able to prevail in Upper Germany because Luther's followers abandoned his more liberal ideas regarding the relation of church and state. They fell back on a more
"medieval" solution which was more attractive to the cities. But
in contrast to the period when the "Reform tradition" was dominant, the communal idea in Upper Germany now went into
permanent decline.

2.

Thus the basic structure of the free cities changed. During the
sixteenth century their glory waned in the Southwest, indeed, in
all of Germany. The Reformation had only retarded the slow
breakdown of the old city community; it had not been able to stop
it. The burghers no longer felt bound to each other or to the city.
As early as the crises of the mid-sixteenth century, this disintegra-
tion had gone so far even in Upper Germany that patricians began
to conspire against their own towns.[40] Gradually city dwellers
changed from participating citizens, responsible for the vigor of
the commonwealth, into mere subjects, owing obedience to the
city government;[41] and the city governments in turn no longer saw
themselves as instruments of the urban community. A rampant
nepotism often seized control, and men worked only to fill their
own pockets.[42] At Biberach the city fathers ceremoniously called

Braun, *Orthodoxie und Pietismus in Memmingen* (Munich, 1935), the
"Reformed" impulses of the ecclesiastical establishment of the imperial
cities shines through.
40. For Lindau, see Wolfart, *Lindau am Bodensee*, pp. 366 f. For Biberach,
see G. Luz, *Beiträge zur Geschichte der ehemaligen Reichsstadt Biberach*
(1876), p. 146. In contrast, four council members at Ulm who sympathized
with Catholicism became convinced in the course of a long dispute that
they should bow to the majority even in ecclesiastical questions. Fritz,
Ulmische Kirchengeschichte, pp. 91 ff.
41. Unfortunately there is no penetrating study of the inner history of the
German and especially the Upper German citizenry in the sixteenth century
of the sort that H. Schmidt, *Städtechroniken*, for example, offers for the
late Middle Ages. The essay by E. von Ranke, "Der Interessenkreis des
deutschen Bürgers im 16. Jahrhundert," *Vierteljahrsschrift für Sozial- und
Wirtschaftsgeschichte* 20 (1928): 474–90, has so narrow a range of sources
and makes so few distinctions that one cannot simply adopt his illuminating results.
42. F. Bothe, *Beiträge zur Wirtschafts- und Sozialgeschichte der Reichsstadt Frankfurt* (Leipzig, 1906), pp. 47 ff., relates some impressive examples from the imperial city of Frankfurt.

themselves the *Magistratus aristocraticus* while labeling the burghers "common rabble."[43] In 1558 the Council of Ulm began using the title of "magistrates instituted by God."[44] Their lordships of Hamburg climbed even higher when they explained in 1602 that even if a government were tyrannical, the subjects still had no right of opposition or revolt since such a government would be a punishment from the Almighty for their sins.[45]

Even previous opponents of the absolutist concept of the state were now attracted to it. Luther's ideal of liberating the state from the church, Zwingli's plan for coordinating both powers, and other teachings of the Reformation were falsified by their second-rate successsors into a reinforcement of the state.[46] Just as, under the influence of Bodin, even the Swiss began to doubt the efficacy of their federated form of government,[47] so too imperial cities of Germany strove to adapt themselves to these new ideas. The imperial cities saw this trend as painful but necessary for withstanding the growing competition of the princely states.[48] Actually,

43. Pfeiffer, "Das Ringen um die Parität," pp. 48, 41.

44. Naujoks, *Obrigkeitsgedanke*, p. 159. Of course, these are particularly crass examples for Upper German circumstances, and one can detect for decades the resistance of the communities everywhere to such pretensions. In Ulm in 1559 Emperor Ferdinand had reason to complain that the old custom of the common oath of the citizenry on the Oath Day had reappeared. Fritz, *Ulmische Kirchengeschichte*, p. 79; Naujoks, *Obrigkeitsgedanke*, p. 116. And a distant reflection of the old communal thinking could be detected even in 1791 when this city replied to imperial summons for measures against revolutionary France by stating that after all it, too, was a republic. Bader, *Reichsstädte*, p. 64.

45. Quoted by G. L. von Maurer, *Geschichte der Stadtverfassung in Deutschland* (Erlangen, 1871), p. 186.

46. This had been shown for Luther in the classic essay of Karl Holl, "Luther und das landesherrliche Kirchenregiment," *Zeitschrift für Theologie und Kirche* 21 (1911), Ergänzungsheft I, pp. 1–60; also in *Gesammelte Aufsätze zur Kirchengeschichte*, 6th ed. (Tübingen, 1932), 1:279–325. For the change in the Zwinglian conception of the state during the sixteenth century, see the book by H. Kressner, *Schweizer Ursprünge des anglikanischen Staatskirchentums* (Gütersloh, 1953), as well as that by R. Wesel-Roth, "Thomas Erastus. Ein Beitrag zur Geschichte der reformierten Kirche und zur Lehre der Staatssouveränität" (Diss., Freiburg i. B., 1954), pp. 90 ff.

47. This is impressively shown by P. Stadler, "Vom eidgenössischen Staatsbewusstsein und Staatensystem um 1600," *Revue Suisse d'Histoire* 8 (1958): 1–20.

48. The struggle between city and territory in the later years of the sixteenth century is graphically depicted in two recent, very different ex-

whenever the imperial cities did survive to the end of the old empire, it was due more to their weakness than to anything else. Their economic power went into permanent decline from the sixteenth century onward.[49] Henceforth they were a less tempting prey, and with the Peace of Westphalia their legal position was reinforced by new guarantees.[50] After 1550 the spiritual center of Germany shifted rapidly away from the imperial cities and away from southern Germany to the princely courts of northern and central Germany.

The impressive theology of the first city reformers was not passed on to a loyal or thoughtful generation on German soil,[51] but rather to Calvin in Geneva. Expanding from Geneva it conquered new regions and different conditions and set in motion those profound changes whose historical effects are still alive.[52] The Reformation produced, in the thoughtful words of Hermann Heimpel, "a frenzy of obedience in the course of German political history, . . . [and a] frenzy of freedom in the course of Western

---

amples: K. Friedland, *Der Kampf der Stadt Lüneberg mit ihren Landesherren* (Hildesheim, 1953), and E. Naujoks, "Reichsfreiheit und Wirtschaftsrivalität. Eine Studie zur Auseinandersetzung Esslingens mit Württemberg im 16. Jahrhundert," *Zeitschrift für württembergische Landesgeschichte* 16 (1957): 279–302.

49. During the Thirty Years' War most of them lost their wealth, which was sometimes considerable. Rörig, *Die europäische Stadt,* p. 125. Augsburg declined between 1600 and 1650 from 44,000 inhabitants to 21,000. Bader, *Reichsstädte,* p. 54. Between 1455 and the nineteenth century even Nuremberg did not need to expand its city boundaries. G. Schmoller, *Das Städtewesen in älterer Zeit* (Bonn, 1922), p. 88. The only exceptions were the large coastal cities of North Germany and especially Hamburg which remained an important port of entry. See H. Mauersberg, *Wirtschafts- und Sozialgeschichte zentraleuropäischer Städte in neurer Zeit* (Göttingen, 1960).

50. At that time they finally gained the right to participate and vote in the Imperial Diet.

51. For successors of Zwingli in Zurich, especially for Gualter, cf. Kressner, *Schweizer Ursprünge,* and Wesel-Roth, "Thomas Erastus." The curious church history of Bremen at the end of the sixteenth century, to which J. Moltmann has created new avenues of approach in recent years (especially in his *Christoph Pezel und der Calvinismus in Bremen* [Bremen, 1958]) is unique in German Protestantism and therefore need not be considered here.

52. "Calvinist political thought helped more than any other tendency of the time to prevent a full victory of absolutism, and to prepare the way for constitutional and even republican ideas." H. Baron, "Calvinist Republicanism in its Historical Roots," *Church History* 8 (1939): 41.

European history."[53] The point of departure for this double development is the breakup of the German Estates during the sixteenth century.

53. H. Heimpel, *Der Mensch in seiner Gegenwart. Sieben historische Essais* (Göttingen, 1954), p. 156.